Integrating Cultural Resources Information into a Historical GIS for the Tower House Historical District, Whiskeytown National Recreation Area, California:

Final Report

Natural Resource Technical Report NPS/KLMN/NRTR — 2010/352

Lorin Groshong

Southern Oregon University
1250 Siskiyou Blvd.
Ashland, OR 97520

Ryan Reid, Research Assistant

Southern Oregon University
1250 Siskiyou Blvd.
Ashland, OR 97520

Sean Mohren, Network Data Manager

Klamath Inventory & Monitoring Network
National Park Service
1250 Siskiyou Blvd.
Ashland, OR 97520

July 2010

U.S. Department of the Interior
National Park Service
Natural Resource Program Center
Fort Collins, Colorado

The National Park Service, Natural Resource Program Center publishes a range of reports that address natural resource topics of interest and applicability to a broad audience in the National Park Service and others in natural resource management, including scientists, conservation and environmental constituencies, and the public.

The Natural Resource Technical Report Series is used to disseminate results of scientific studies in the physical, biological, and social sciences for both the advancement of science and the achievement of the National Park Service mission. The series provides contributors with a forum for displaying comprehensive data that are often deleted from journals because of page limitations.

All manuscripts in the series receive the appropriate level of peer review to ensure that the information is scientifically credible, technically accurate, appropriately written for the intended audience, and designed and published in a professional manner.

This report received informal peer review by subject-matter experts who were not directly involved in the collection, analysis, or reporting of the data.

Views, statements, findings, conclusions, recommendations, and data in this report do not necessarily reflect views and policies of the National Park Service, U.S. Department of the Interior. Mention of trade names or commercial products does not constitute endorsement or recommendation for use by the U.S. Government.

This report is available from The Klamath Inventory and Monitoring Network (http://science.nature.nps.gov/im/units/klmn) and the Natural Resource Publications Management website (http://www.nature.nps.gov/publications/NRPM).

Please cite this publication as:

Groshong, L. C., R. D. Reid, and S. R. Mohren. 2010. Integrating cultural resources information into a historical GIS for the Tower House Historical District, Whiskeytown National Recreation Area, California: Final Report. Natural Resource Technical Report NPS/KLMN/NRTR—2010/352. National Park Service, Fort Collins, Colorado.

TIC Number: 611/104871

Contents

Figures

Appendices

Executive Summary

This report presents the results of a 6 month project, which created an Integrated Geographic Information System for Cultural Resources in the Tower House Historic District of Whiskeytown National Recreation Area. The Tower House Historic District and associated Archeological District are in the National Register of Historic Places. Funding for this Geographic Information System (GIS) project came from the Pacific West Region office of the National Park Service (NPS) under PMIS project number 139248 (Appendix A).

The National Park Service has service-wide requirements for management of cultural resources. The ability to fulfill these requirements can be greatly enhanced through the use of GIS technology. For many projects that may impact cultural resources, parks must review spatial information including locations of archeological sites, historic structures, cultural landscapes, ethnographic resources, and the extent of completed archeological surveys. Many park units still maintain base maps for archeological sites in paper format. In addition, other cultural resource data may exist in various physical and digital formats. All of these data are consulted regularly and need to be in an easy-to-use accessible format, as has been accomplished in this project.

This GIS project is designed to incorporate a variety of GIS data being managed by the NPS including cultural resources, park maintained facilities and utilities, and historical land-use and ownership data layers. These GIS data layers are dynamically linked to ancillary data including records and reports in PDF format, tabular data in spreadsheets, online databases such as the List of Classified Structures (LCS), and digital photographs so they can be easily accessed. Metadata and attribute information have been designed to expedite NHPA and NEPA compliance, year-end reporting to Congress, GPRA, and the State Historic Preservation Office (SHPO). The data in this project also meet Cultural Resource Base Map management requirements (NPS 28), achieve park level management goals (GMP and Fire Management Plan), expedite cultural resources project-related record searches, and promote efficient map production for archeological site records and reports.

Acknowledgements

We thank the employees of Whiskeytown National Recreation Area for taking time out of their work days to familiarize us with the Tower House Historical District (THHD). We would especially like to give thanks to Barbara Alberti, Jennifer Gibson, Clinton Kane, Joe Svinarich, and Russ Weatherbee for all their time and effort. Frank Moreno and Clinton Kane were kind enough to give us a tour of the THHD and described much of the history of the area. We also appreciate the technical assistance with servers and database administration from Dave Best and Jay Flaming. Bess Perry from the Klamath Network provided editing assistance.

Introduction

Project Description

Whiskeytown National Recreation Area (WHIS) has specific needs for mapping, data organization, and integration for the Tower House Historic District (Figure 1). For many projects that may impact cultural resources, parks must review spatial information including locations of archeological sites, historic structures, cultural landscapes, ethnographic resources, and the extent of completed archeological surveys. In the past, data on cultural resources were held either on the fire archeologist's computer or in museum collections that were difficult to access. Other GIS data were held on personal computers as well, which limited the ability of anyone to access all the layers of data needed to create a complete map of the region. This project's main goal was to integrate these GIS and ancillary data for the Tower House Historic District so that the employees at Whiskeytown National Recreation Area can more easily map the region, complete project-related record searches, develop work plans for National Park Service archeologists, and develop contract Scopes of Work.

An integrated cultural resources data structure that includes GIS and ancillary data has been developed for the Tower House Historical District (THHD) in Whiskeytown National Recreation Area. This project incorporates various types of GIS data being managed by the National Park Service including cultural resources, park-maintained facilities and utilities, and historical land-use and ownership. GIS data layers have been dynamically linked to ancillary data, including records and reports in PDF format, tabular data in spreadsheets, online databases such as the List of Classified Structures (LCS), and digital photographs. Metadata and attribute information for GIS data layers have been designed to expedite National Historic Preservation Act (NHPA), National Environmental Protection Agency (NEPA), State Historic Preservation Office (SHPO), and Government Performance Results Act (GPRA) compliance. The project has also been designed to expedite year-end reporting to Congress, achieve park level management goals (General Management Plan and Fire Management Plan), facilitate cultural resources project-related record searches, and promote efficient map production for archeological site records and reports.

In addition to the direct benefits of this project to the staff at WHIS, this project also works to serve the needs of the Klamath Network (KLMN). Organizing the park's GIS data in a manner that ensures everyone is using and updating the same data layers helps make certain the Network has the most up-to-date information to use as part of our inventory and monitoring program. This project was managed through a task agreement (J9W88040020) between the KLMN and Southern Oregon University.

Study Area

Whiskeytown is located within the territorial boundaries of the Wintu people, who utilized the area for hundreds of years before the arrival of Euro-Americans in the 19th century. Ten prehistoric archeological sites are currently listed in the National Register of Historic Places as part of the Tower House Archeological District (NPS 1999). In addition to the Archeological District, the Tower House Historic District, listed on the National Register of Historic Places in 1973, encompasses 20 acres and includes 16 structures. Its two primary residents, Levi Tower and Charles Camden, contributed significant developments in commerce, transportation, agriculture, and industry in northern California for two decades following the discovery of gold in 1848. The district includes the Camden House, which has been preserved and stabilized; the tenant house, which is currently used as staff housing; a barn; outbuildings; a bridge; an extensive irrigation system; and the El Dorado Mine and Stamp Mill (NPS 1999)

Methods

Project work consisted of a series of meetings interspersed with digital mapping work. Stakeholders, including regional and local managers, oversaw different aspects of the project. At the national level, a Cultural Resources Data Standard is in the process of being finalized. Jay Flaming in the Pacific West Region office in Seattle, Washington incorporated Whiskeytown Cultural GIS data into the standardized ArcSDE Database structure. At the park level, a server was transferred from Redwood National Park to Whiskeytown National Recreation Area in October 2009 by David Best. Russ Weatherbee then transferred park GIS base-data such as boundaries, modern air photos, transportation, and utilities to the server. The main product of this GIS project is an ArcMap project (.mxd) that connects to these various data sources and delivers the data in a single user-friendly mapping environment.

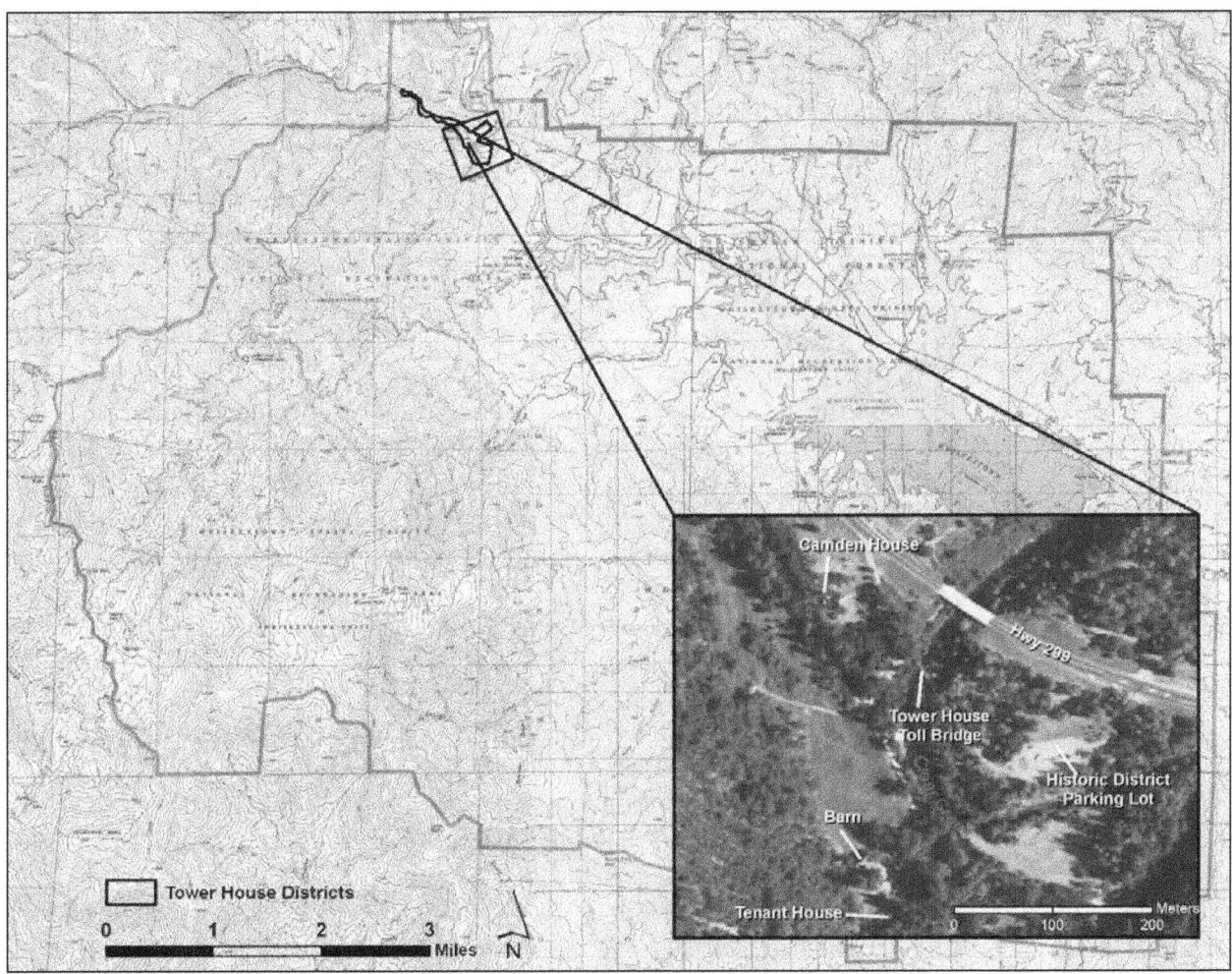

Figure 1. Map of Whiskeytown National Recreation Area, showing the location of the Tower House Historic and Archeological Districts

Project Management

Five meetings were held throughout the project to ensure that park and regional staff was involved at every stage of production, and that data were being incorporated from all stakeholders.

An introductory meeting was held on August 5, 2009. The goal of this meeting was to provide an overview of the project and to discuss major aspects of the project with the stakeholders. Items that were discussed included: objectives, timelines, deliverables, standards, boundaries, data structure, data sources, and departmental needs. Final products resulting from discussions in the first meeting were to have: (1) digital data organized according to all appropriate data standards and in a file structure that could be used by the park as a permanent GIS file structure; (2) a final report and poster for presentations describing file structure, data standards, and how they would address the needs of the park; and (3) a complete ArcGIS.mxd file in an easily accessible format for use by park staff. It was also determined that the final Tower House Historic District GIS product would connect to the Cultural Resources GIS data from the standardized regional database.

The second meeting occurred on August 17, 2009, and was used to tour THHD and to capture GPS data of utilities, including water pipes and buried power lines in the area. Frank Moreno guided Southern Oregon University and KLMN staff to the location of known utilities that were not previously in a digital format. The resulting GPS data were the only new data collected for this project.

A third meeting, on October 19-20, 2009, was held to set up the Whiskeytown server, which was to become the storage location for this project, and to complete a status check on the progress of the project. A preliminary project location on the server was created so that designated park and regional staff could access the utility and progress of the project. Completing this early in the process gave all stakeholders the opportunity to review project materials while they were being developed. During this meeting, it was also decided that this project would utilize the Environmental Systems Research Institute's (ESRI) ArcSDE technology and replication capabilities to share GIS data between network parks, the KLMN, and regional offices.

A fourth meeting was held on December 19, 2009, to demonstrate the draft of the final product so it could be critiqued by Whiskeytown staff. Remote desktop was used to connect to the WHIS server, and ArcMap was used to demo the final map project. The cultural resources data were connected to the regional SDE database and follow the new national Cultural Resources GIS data standards (Appendix C). This database will continue to be administered at the regional level. The project at Whiskeytown connects to the database seamlessly, and as a result, users do not need to know anything about SDE technology to view and utilize the data. Local Whiskeytown base data (roads, trails, DEM, DOQQ, etc.) still needed to be put in a final organization on the server. Hyperlinks were active in the ArcMap project and several features were selected to demonstrate the ability to click on a feature and view materials related to that feature (e.g., photographs, online documentation, PDF documents). Many features have multiple ancillary products linked to them and it is possible to choose the product you want to view. Additionally, a sample mapbook product was demonstrated and determined to not be useful for this small of an area.

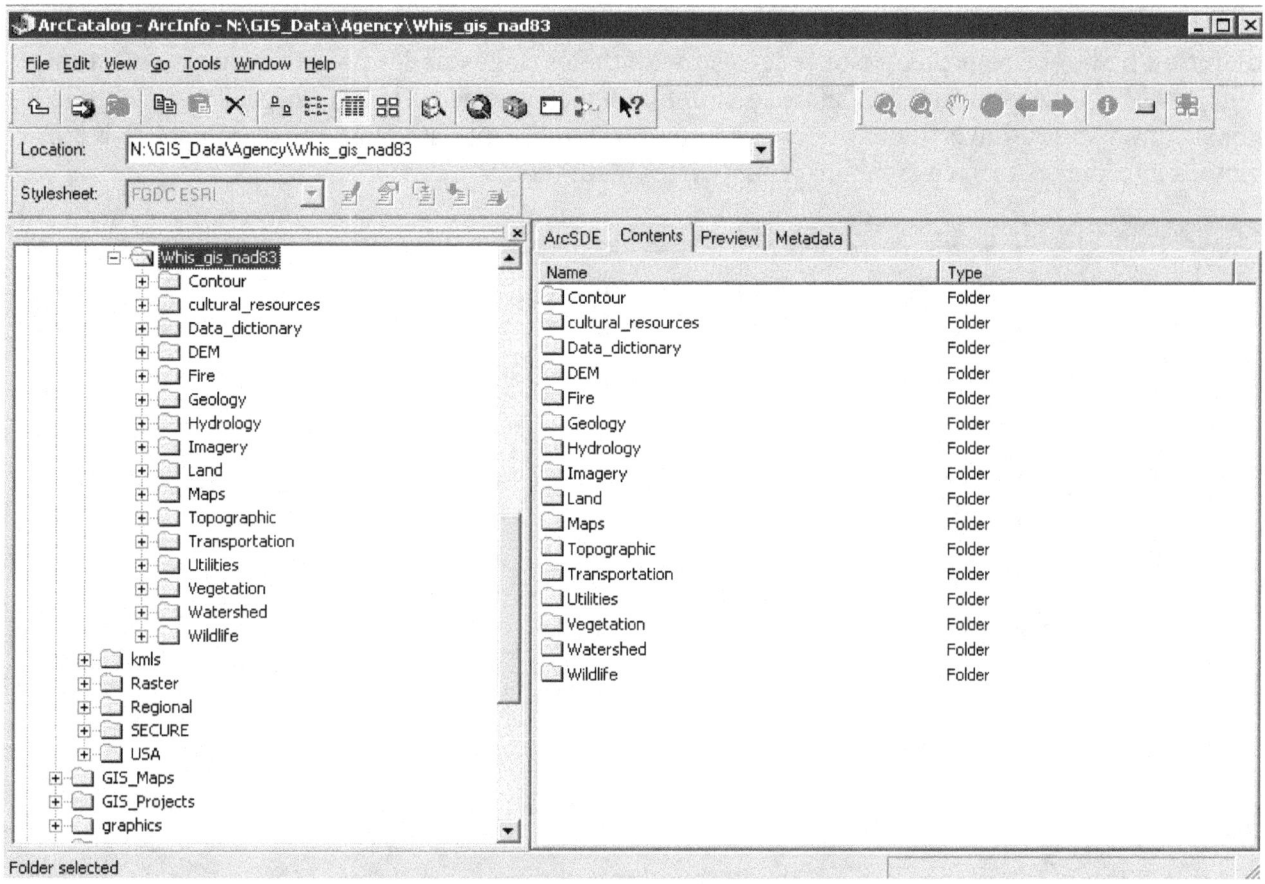

Figure 2. File structure for GIS data on the new Whiskeytown Server.

The final meeting on January 22, 2010, was held to discuss the location of the project and data on the WHIS server. After the meeting, the ArcMap project, GIS shapefiles, and layer files were moved to the server following the standardized format (Figure 2). It took a few more weeks for all of the local park data to get placed on the server and links between the THHD project and the local base data were continually updated until this process was complete. It is expected that new base data may be added to the WHIS server in the future and an SOP has been written that details how to add new data to the THHD project when needed (Appendix D)

Data Collection and Organization

This project primarily acquired and organized existing datasets from multiple computers at Whiskeytown National Recreation Area, as well as including the ArcSDE data hosted at the Pacific West Region Office.

Local (WHIS) Datasets: Base GIS Data, Cultural GIS Data, and Ancillary (non-GIS) Data:

After receiving gigabytes of data from various stakeholders at WHIS, we began filtering through data to organize the information and to help find pieces of data that would be relevant to the project. Once all relevant data had been located and duplicates removed, we created a folder structure for the project (Figure 3). In some cases, files were renamed for easier identification. Much of the original data from Whiskeytown were in a geographic projection that used a historical datum (NAD27) or had no projection defined. The majority of the data for this project therefore had to be re-projected or redefined with the current standard North American Datum 1983 (NAD83). A personal geodatabase structure was constructed to help organize the data in a consistent manner. Layerfiles were created out of the relevant data from the geodatabase feature classes as a means to save symbology associated with the data.

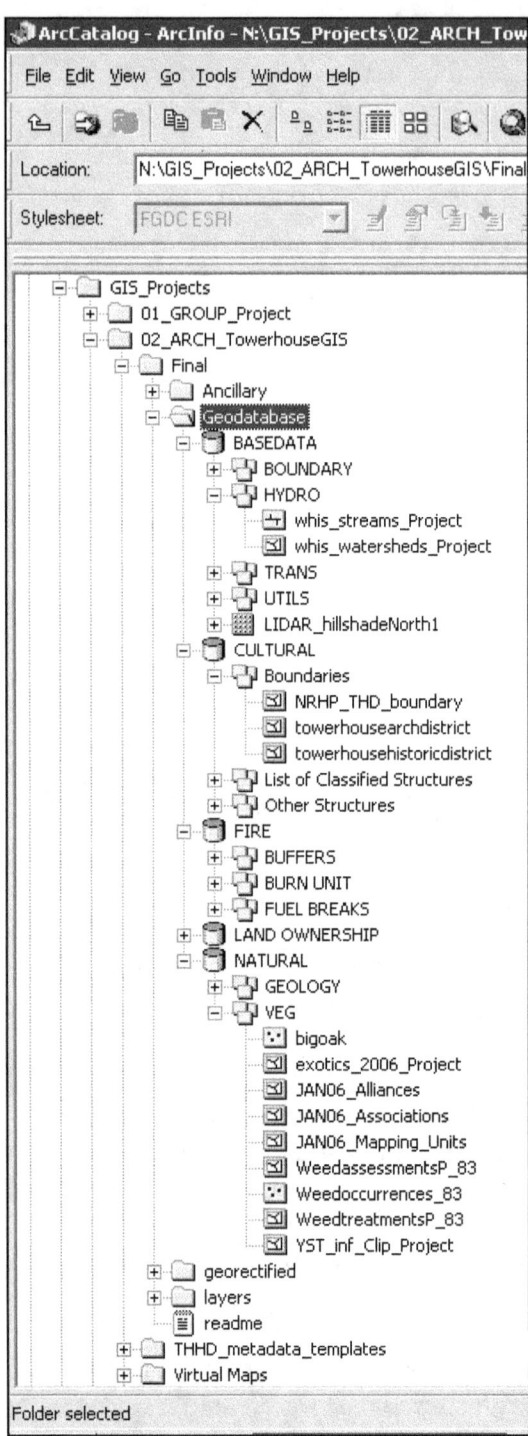

Figure 3. Temporary project file structure for data organization purposes.

Georectification of Photographs and Report Maps

Historic air photos and report maps were georectified to the project area when features could be identified on a georectified image (Figure 4). This process aligns features on the image to the identical features on the underlying base map, warping the image as needed to conform to the more accurate base map. As part of the folder structure described above, there is a georectified folder containing all photos as well as the tie-points used for georectification. In the metadata for the air photos, Root Mean Square (RMS) error was recorded. All photos were georectified with an RMS error of less than 10 m. The Tower House District was the focus of georectification on all images so the image is most accurate around the Tower House District and increasingly distorted farther away from the Tower House District.

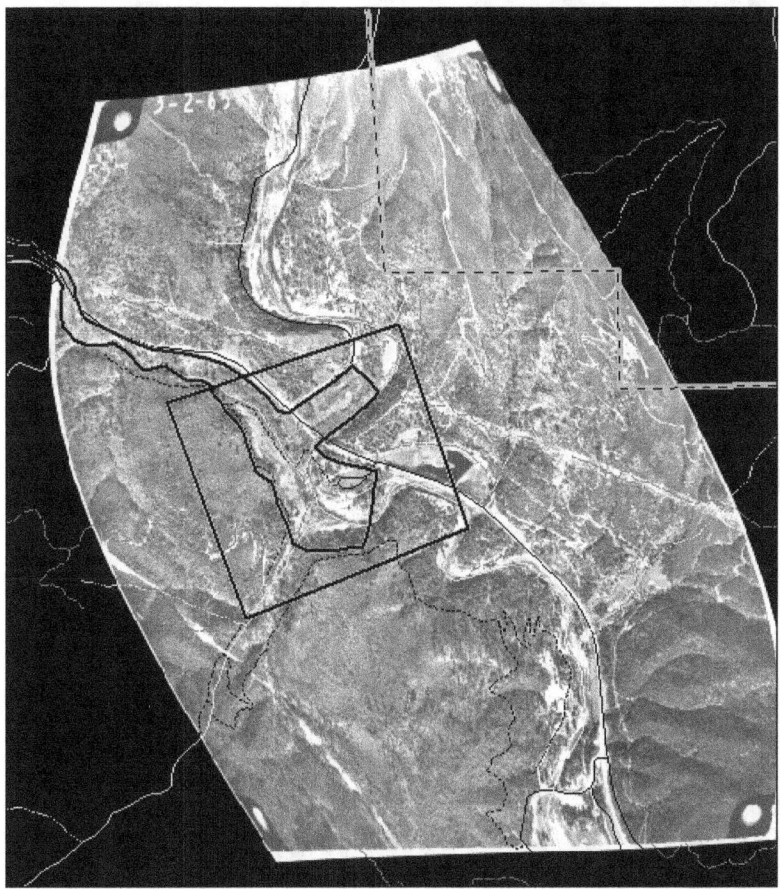

Figure 4. Historic air photo from project after georectification.

In order to create new datasets of historic buildings and features not previously included in GIS data, building footprints were digitized from base maps in the Cultural Landscape Report (Historical Research Associates 2001). This was done by co-registering historic base maps with a NAIP 2005 Digital Orthophoto Quad (DOQ) imagery. Once known features on the scanned map matched up with the DOQ, new features found on the base map could be traced. The tracings represent the approximate location of those features during the time period specified on the base map (Figure 5). These time periods were entered into the attributes and metadata for the new features as well.

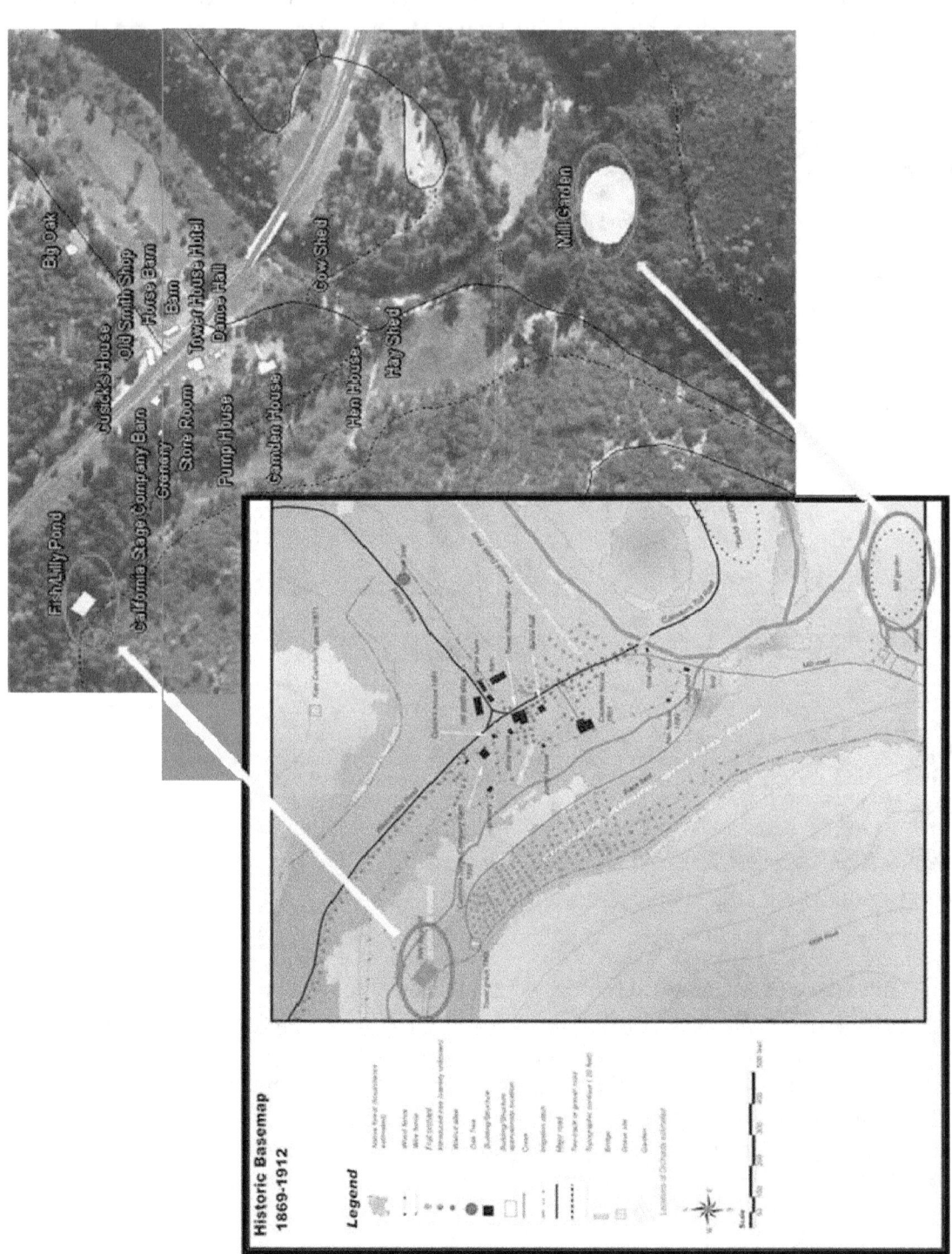

Figure 5. Digitizing historical data from Cultural Landscape Report images.

8

Metadata

For any new data that were created as part of this project (GPS or digitized), full metadata records were developed (Figure 6). For data originally from Whiskeytown, a template was created that requires a knowledgeable party to complete sections like the Abstract, Purpose, and Supplementary Information. Whiskeytown personnel are responsible for completion and upkeep of those aspects of the metadata that require their experience and knowledge of the region.

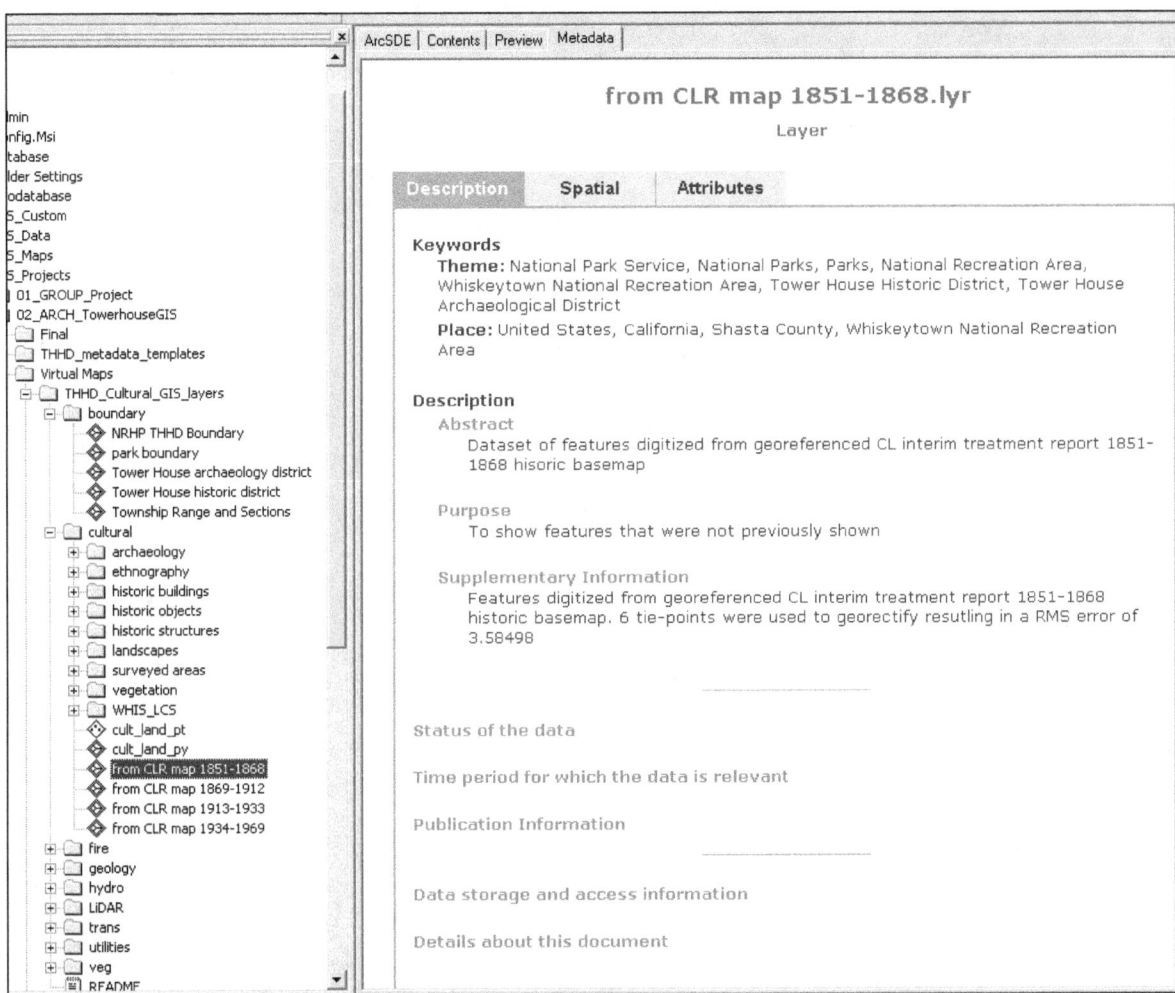

Figure 6. Example metadata

Pacific West Region ArcSDE Data: Cultural Resources GIS Data

ArcSDE data created by Jay Flaming, PWR Seattle, were also imported into the THHD ArcMap project. There were two primary reasons for using SDE data for this project: (1) to maintain a data standard (Appendix C) for all Cultural Resources data network-wide; and (2) to prevent the problems that arise from users creating and saving duplicates of data to multiple folders. When the SDE data are updated by an administrator, the SDE data in the project are automatically updated.

The following datasets were converted to SDE format: Cultural Landscapes, Historic Buildings, Historic Objects, Historic Structures, Archaeology, Ethnography, Surveyed Areas, and Orchard Vegetation.

9

The connection to this regional database system was set up by Dave Best, Redwood National Park, who will continue to administer the database connections. Once connected to the database, the data were added to the ArcMap project. The layers these data comprise now behave like the shapefiles that Whiskeytown employees are familiar with.

Results

Major Project Accomplishments:

1. A server for GIS data moved from Redwood National Park to Whiskeytown National Recreation Area and put into use. This allows all GIS data users to access the same GIS files, rather than having different versions in use on different computers. The server should house the most up-to-date versions of GIS shapefiles in NAD83 UTM Zone 10N coordinate system. Russ Weatherbee is the current local administrator of the server.

2. Structured Cultural Resources ArcSDE data successfully added to final ArcMap project. All Cultural Resource GIS data in the final ArcMap project are hosted and updated at a regional level, ensuring that everyone is using identical datasets. Additionally, all Cultural Resource GIS data follow the new national data standards. Any updates made to the data at a regional level will automatically be changed in the local data as well.

3. Ancillary data (hundreds of reports, historical photographs, and other scanned documents) are hyperlinked to geographic features on map so that non-GIS documents can be opened from the GIS map window (Figure 7). A Standard Operation Procedure manual has been created, ensuring that users at WHIS can easily and properly add documents and photos to the project.

4. A detailed list of data included in this ArcMap project can be found in Appendix B. However, general data includes:

   - District and park boundaries
   - Hydrology
   - Current transportation networks
   - Historical transportation networks
   - Modern and historic utilities
   - Fire data (fuel breaks, buffers and burn units)
   - Modern vegetation maps
   - Geology maps
   - Digital Raster Graphic (DRG – USGS topographic map)
   - LiDAR hillshade
   - Scanned and georeferenced historic maps (General Land Office Surveys [GLO 1869], Metsker, CalTrans, Bureau of Land Management, and historic mining and ownership maps)
   - Digitized historic maps (digitized objects and buildings not seen in existing data)
   - Scanned and georeferenced maps from reports and historical narratives (Manuel 1977, Baker 1984 and 1990, Davis-King 1997, Bevill 1999, Fitzgerald 2003, NPS 2008)
   - Scanned and georectified historic air photos
   - Data in Cultural Resources GIS data standard (from ArcSDE):
     - Cultural landscapes
     - Historic structures (from List of Classified Structures)
     - Historic objects
     - Historic buildings

- Ethnographic data
- Archaeology
- Surveyed areas

The combination of these data layers allows users to accomplish most, if not all, of the geographical tasks that might be required for the THHD region, including creating detailed base maps of the region, querying locations of utilities relative to cultural resources, and observing changes to the region over time.

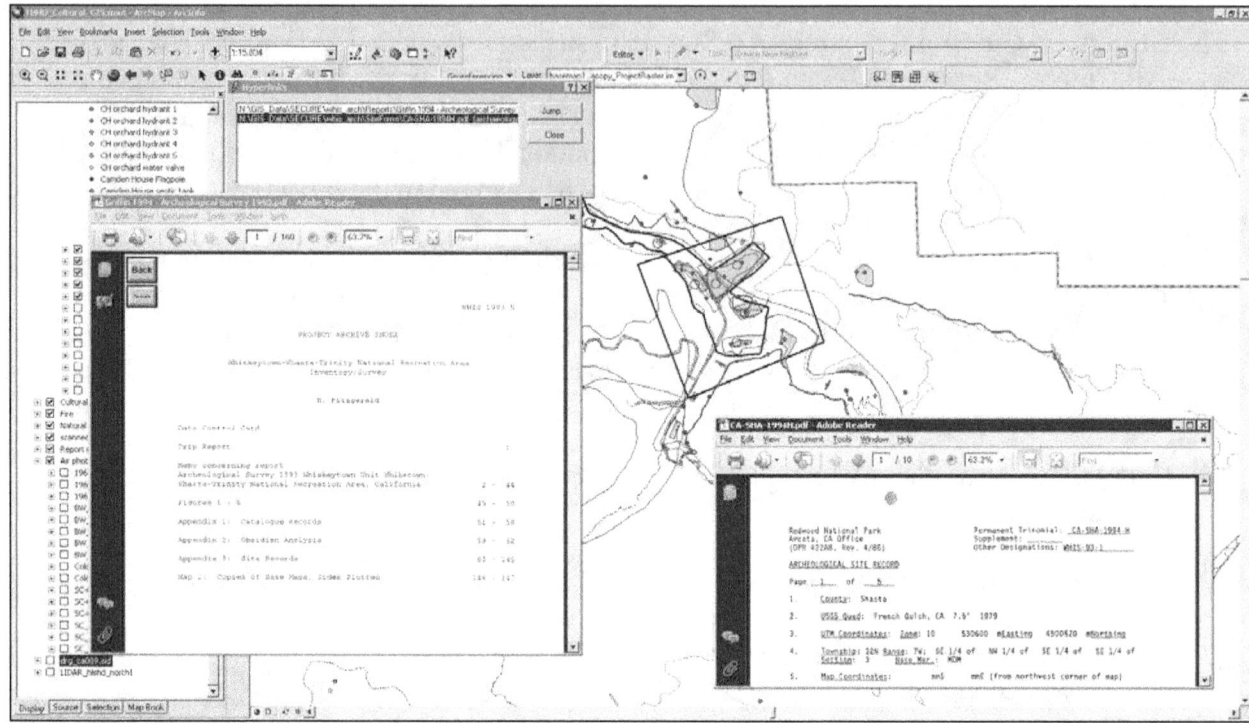

Figure 7. Hyperlinked documents available from the ArcMap project by clicking the hyperlink button (a lightning bolt - circled in red, above).

Discussion

This project provides users at Whiskeytown National Recreation Area with a single document that connects them to the geographic and ancillary data about THHD. Through this map document, users are able to view any base data on the GIS server, open cultural resource datasets that follow national standards, and click on features in the map to see the ancillary documents pertaining to the selected feature. In gathering data for the project, the park was inspired to compile their own GIS data on the new server as well, which was then integrated into the existing project data.

As a result, Whiskeytown National Recreation Area has a single repository of their geographic and ancillary data in a highly functional format, which meets national standards, is easily updatable at both the local and regional levels, and ensures that park employees are seeing and using the same data. This will greatly enhance their ability to meet the National Park Service's requirements for management of cultural resources.

Management Recommendations

This project has been designed in a manner so individuals with limited training will be able to create maps and examine GIS and non-GIS data associated with the THHD. The park staff should work to ensure that all staff members who may find having access to these data useful (Cultural, Natural, Maintenance, etc.) are aware of the project, understand how the project can be used, and receive adequate training on how to use the ArcMap project.

In addition, as with any GIS project, if the data are not continuously managed and updated, then the project will become outdated and less useful. To ensure this does not happen, WHIS has setup a server to manage their GIS data. It is important to make certain staff understand why storing data on the server (versus their personal computers) is important. Training should be received for all people using or managing GIS data on how to access the data on the server, store data on the server, and on how to update data currently on the server. Making certain a plan is in place on how to manage and use the GIS data will help ensure this project as well as all GIS projects developed at the park will be accurate, consistent, and up-to-date now and into the future.

Literature Cited

Baker, S. 1984. Archaeological investigations in the Tower House District, Whiskeytown Unit of the Whiskeytown-Shasta-Trinity National Recreation Area, Shasta County, California. Submitted to the National Park Service, Western Region, San Francisco, California by Archaeological Consultants, Oakland, California. August 1984.

Baker, S. 1990. Archaeological excavations at CA-SHA-479 and CA-SHA-195, Whiskeytown Unit, Whiskeytown-Shasta-Trinity National Recreation Area, Shasta County, California. Submitted to the National Park Service, Western Region, San Francisco, California by Archaeological/Historical Consultants, Oakland, California. April 1990.

Bevill, R. 1999. The archaeology of the Tower House Site, CA-SHA-192/479/H, Shasta County, California: 2-Sha-299, P.M. 8.5/9.0. Submitted to California Department of Transportation Environmental Branch, Sacramento, California, in partial satisfaction of Contract No. 43Y529. April 1999.

Davis-King, S. 1997. Bringing water to the garden: A description of two ditches in the Tower House Historic District, Whiskeytown National Recreation Area, Shasta County, California. Submitted to the National Park Service, San Francisco, California, 1997.

Fitzgerald, K. 2003. Cultural Landscapes Inventory (Part 1): Camden House Historic District, Whiskeytown-Shasta-Trinity National Recreation Area. National Park Service.

General Land Office. 1869. Partial surveys of T32N R7W and T33N R7W, 1869. Bureau of Land Management, Sacramento, California.

Historical Research Associates, Inc. 2001. Cultural landscape report, Part I for Tower House Historic District in the Whiskeytown Unit of the Whiskeytown-Shasta-Trinity National Recreation Area, Shasta County, California. Prepared for the National Park Service by Historical Research Associates, Inc., Amphion Environmental, Inc., December 2001.

Manuel, D. W. 1977. Archaeological survey of selected areas within the Tower House NRA, and Irrigation Districts, Whiskeytown NRA, Highway 299W, between PM 7.7 – PM 8.7, seven miles east of the Trinity County line to Clear Creek: E.A. 034411. Submitted by Donald W. Manuel. August 25, 1977.

National Park Service. 1999. General Management Plan and Environmental Impact Statement: Whiskeytown Unit, Shasta County, California. Whiskeytown Unit, Whiskeytown-Shasta_Trinity National Recreation Area, Pacific West Region, June 1999.

National Park Service 2008. Tower House Historic District cultural landscape interim treatment report. Whiskeytown Unit, Whiskeytown-Shasta_Trinity National Recreation Area, Pacific West Region, 2008.

Appendix A: PMIS 139248

Project Title: Integrate Cultural Resource Information into Historical GIS	**Project Total Cost:** $25,000.00
Park/Unit: Whiskeytown National Recreation Area	**Region:** Pacific West
States: CA	**Congressional District:** CA02
Old Package Number:	**Reference Number:**
Project Type: Non-facility	**Financial System Package Number:** WHIS 139248
Contact Person: Joe Svinarich	**Contact Phone:** 530-242-3458

Project Status - PMIS 139248

Date Created: 11/13/07	**Review Status:** Park-Approved on 12/05/2007
Date of Last Update: 12/07/07	**Updated By:** Barbara N. Alberti

Project Narratives - PMIS 139248

Description

An integrated cultural resources data structure that includes GIS and ancillary data will be developed to include all types of cultural resources managed by the NPS, park maintained facilities and utilities, and historical land-use and ownership data layers. These GIS data layers will be dynamically linked to ancillary data including records and reports in PDF format, tabular data in spreadsheets, on-line databases such as the List of Classified Structures (LCS), and digital photographs. Metadata and attribute information for GIS data layers will be designed to expedite NHPA & NEPA compliance, year-end reporting to Congress, GPRA, and the State Historic Preservation Office (SHPO), meet Cultural Resource Base Map management requirements (NPS 28), achieve park level management goals (GMP and Fire Mgmt. Plan), expedite cultural resources project related record searches, and promote efficient map production for archeological site records and reports.

The NPS has service-wide requirements for management of cultural resources that can be greatly enhanced through the use of GIS technology. For all projects that may impact cultural resources, parks must review spatial information including locations of archeological sites, historic structures, cultural landscapes, ethnographic resources, and the extent of completed archeological surveys. This information is consulted to complete project related record searches, develop work plans for NPS archeologists, and develop contract Scopes of Work. Many park units still maintain base maps for archeological sites in paper format. In addition, other cultural resource data may exist in various physical and digital formats. All of this data is consulted regularly and needs to be in an easy-to-use accessible format as proposed in this project.

Justifications

NPS units have service-wide legal requirements for management of cultural resources that inherently require data management. Development of a functional integrated cultural resources database that incorporates GIS data will allow park units to efficiently address management mandates for cultural resources (NPS 28), NHPA & NEPA compliance (PEPC), Fire Management Plan Goals (rapid assessment), GMP Goals (GPRA reporting), NHPA year-end reporting (annual report to congress and the system-wide archeological inventory program report), and annual NHPA Section 106 report to SHPO.

This project will extend the existing Integrated Cultural Resource Dataset (ICRD) structure originally developed by staff at WACC. Currently Whiskeytown maintains a version of the ICRD that includes GIS data layers for archeological sites, archeological surveys, ethnographic points, and some historical land use and ownership information. This project will expand and standardize existing attribute data and metadata for archeological sites, isolated finds, surveys, and historical structures. It will continue development of historical land-use and ownership GIS data layers based on General Land Office and BLM plats, Metzker & NPS land ownership maps, and other sources. New GIS data layers will be developed for cultural landscapes and their features, ethnographic data, archeological excavations, archeological features, and park structures and utilities.

Development of this type of cultural resources geo-spatial database will result in an invaluable tool for NPS staff conducting cultural resource record searches prior to undertaking making types of projects. This geo-spatial database will also streamline the process and increase the accuracy of service-wide annual reporting requirements. Whiskeytown is one of the few NPS units in the PWR that maintains cultural resource data in digital format. Completion of the geo-spatial database will provide a model that can be used by other NPS units throughout the PWR as an example as they move forward in converting their cultural resources data into digital format.

This project will provide a working model that can be used as an example for PWR and National staff tasked with development of NPS standards for cultural resource GIS data. This project will build on the existing ICRD structure currently in use at several park units in the PWR. GIS data layer attribute information will be developed in a fashion to promote quick and efficient data queries designed specifically to provide information required for the various required year-end reports, expedite literature review for specific project locations, and facilitate site record and report preparation. This will also include development of map templates in ArcGIS to simulate State of California site record formats.

This project will focus on development of a data structure clearly defined in a final report that can be used as a reference for other park units that need an example to initiate similar projects. To ensure completion of the project within acceptable time frames, data will be compiled from various sources and integrated into a working model for the Tower House Cultural Landscape Historic District. Focus on this working model will limit the overall project scope into a manageable area, and provide Whiskeytown with a management tool for the many maintenance projects that occur within the historic district. Specific data layers that are needed for year-end reporting and completing NHPA & NEPA compliance will be fully developed at the park-wide level to address assistance needs in these areas at Whiskeytown. Specific data layers that are needed for year-end reporting and completing NHPA & NEPA compliance will be fully developed at the park-wide level. These include archeological sites and surveys, LCS, ethnographic locations, and CLI boundaries. Associated ancillary data will be organized to allow hyperlinking to the spatial data layers. The remaining GIS layers and ancillary data will be developed as much as possible within the allocated time.

Measurable Results

The proposed project will consist of compiling and processing data for a study area to create a fully functional demonstration model. The area proposed for completion of a demonstration model is the Tower House Cultural Landscape Historic District. Data layers will include one for historical structures based on the NPS List of Classified Structures (LCS), a cultural landscape layer for features associated with the Tower House Historic Landscape District, and historical land use and ownership. A fair amount of ancillary data has been collected that needs to be organized and linked to the existing GIS data layers to complete the geo-spatial database. Air photos from the study area taken over the past 40 years will be orthorectified and integrated into the GIS.

The existing GIS data layers need to be reviewed and updated with additional attribute data to assist cultural resource staff with record searches prior to conducting fieldwork, to document compliance with the National Historic Preservation Act, and to assist with year-end reporting requirements. Additional feature level data layers need to be developed for archeological sites and cultural landscapes.

Work will be completed by hiring a CSU, Chico Geography graduate student with strong background in GIS and data management. Guidance and oversight will be provided by Whiskeytown staff with experience in GIS applications and theory. Park staff will coordinate their efforts with PWR regional GIS staff currently developing cultural resource GIS standards for the PWR. Regional cultural resource staff will also be consulted when developing data structures and GIS data layers for archeology, cultural landscapes, historic structures, and ethnographic resources.

The final results of this project will be summarized in a report that provides a comprehensive overview of the integrated cultural resources data structure complete with a descriptive example of the various GIS data layers that discusses the associated ancillary data and how these can be used to address management requirements such as year-end reporting and completing NHPA & NEPA compliance. A poster suitable for presentation at a conference or publication on the PWR GIS web site will also be prepared.

Project Activities, Assets, Emphasis Areas and GPRA Goals - PMIS 139248

Activities

- Compliance
- Manage Information
- Interpret and Inform
- Planning
- Preservation
- Research
- Study/Evaluation

Assets

- Mineral
- Archeological Resource
- Cultural Landscape
- Ethnographic Resource
- Fences/Walls
- GIS Data
- Historic Structure
- IT Application System
- Maintained Landscape
- Road - Paved
- Road - Unpaved

Emphasis Areas

- Indian Tribe Inclusion
- Partnerships

GPRA Goals and Percent Values

- Historic Structures, 20%
- Park Upland Acres Restored, 20%
- Archeological sites , 20%
- Park Fire Goal, 20%
- Cultural Landscapes, 20%

Project Prioritization Information - PMIS 139248

Unit Priority: 45 **IN FY** 2008	**Unit Priority Band:** MEDIUM

Project Assistance Needs - PMIS 139248

Is Assistance Needed: No	

Related OFS Funding Requests - PMIS 139248

Request ID: 5122	**Request title:** Provide Information Technology and Communications Support
Request ID: 5982	**Request title:** Restore Disturbed Lands

Project Funding Component - PMIS 139248A

Funding Component Title: Integrate Cultural Resource Information into Historical GIS	**Funding Component Request Amount:** $25,000.00
Funding Component Reference Number (Multi-purpose):	**Funding Component Type:** Non-recurring , Not Deferred

Funding Component Description:

Initial Planned FY: 2009	**Requested Funding FY:** 2009
Review Status: Awaiting Park Submission	**Funded Amount:**
Upper-level Review Status:	**Fee-demo Submission Number:**
Formulated FY:	**Funded FY:**
Formulated Program:	**Funded PWE Accounts:**
Formulated Funding Source:	**Funded Funding Source:**

Component Cost Estimates

Estimated By: Barbara Alberti   **Date of Estimate:** 11/13/2007

Estimate in 2008 dollars   Class of Estimate: B

Item	Description	Qty	Unit	Unit Cost	Item Cost
Personnel Services	GS-07 GIS Tech for 14 payperiods.	1	Lump	$21,500.00	$21,500.00
Supplies and Equipment	GIS capable computer ($3,000), PhotoShop software ($500)	1	Lump	$3,500.00	$3,500.00
				Component Funding Request	$25,000.00

Eligible Funding Sources and Funding Priorities

Funding Source	Unit Priority at Formulation	Regional Priority	National Priority	Year Unit-Prioritized
No Eligible Funding Sources Specified				

20

Appendix B: Comprehensive List of Layers in Final Map Product

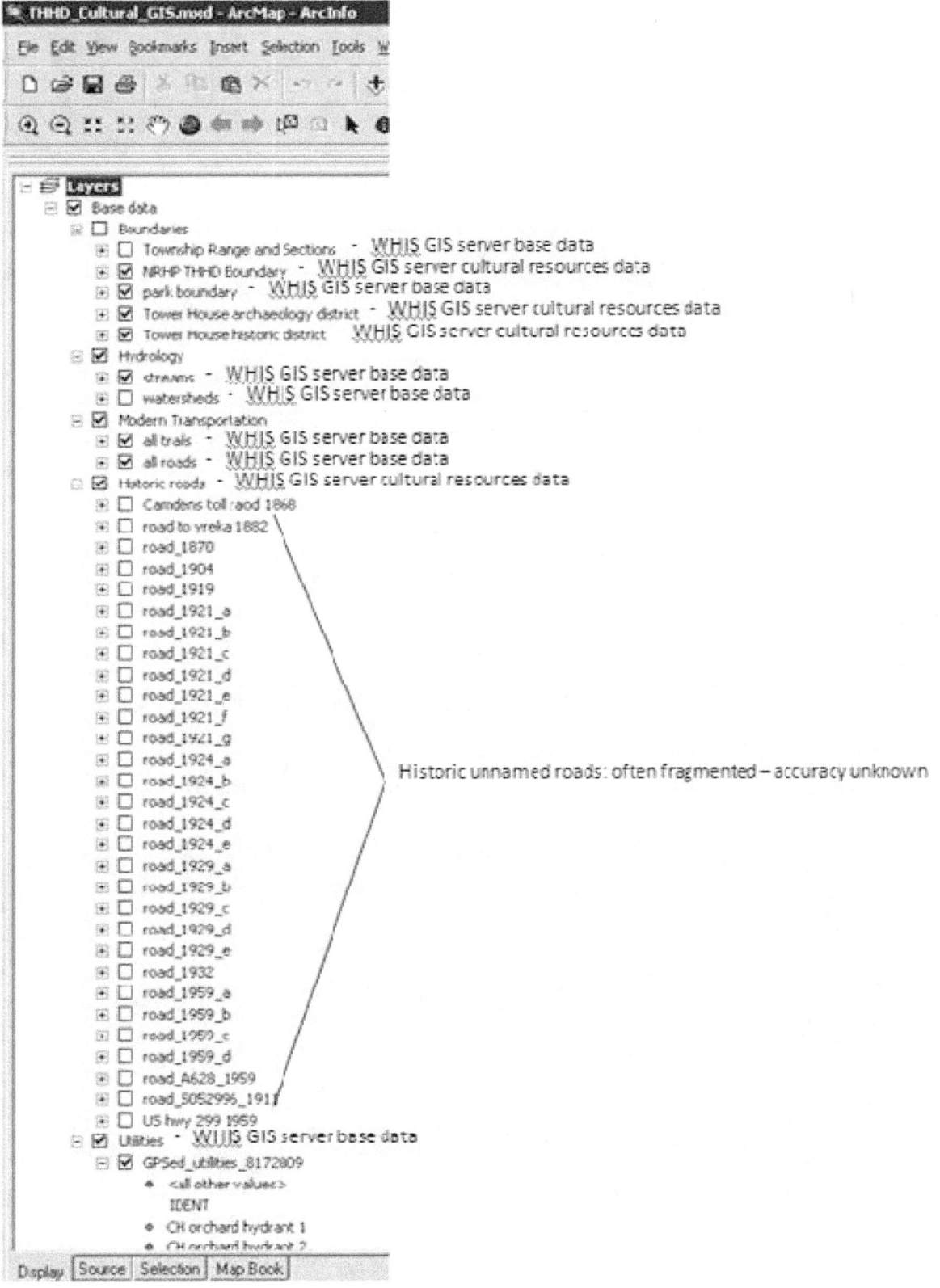

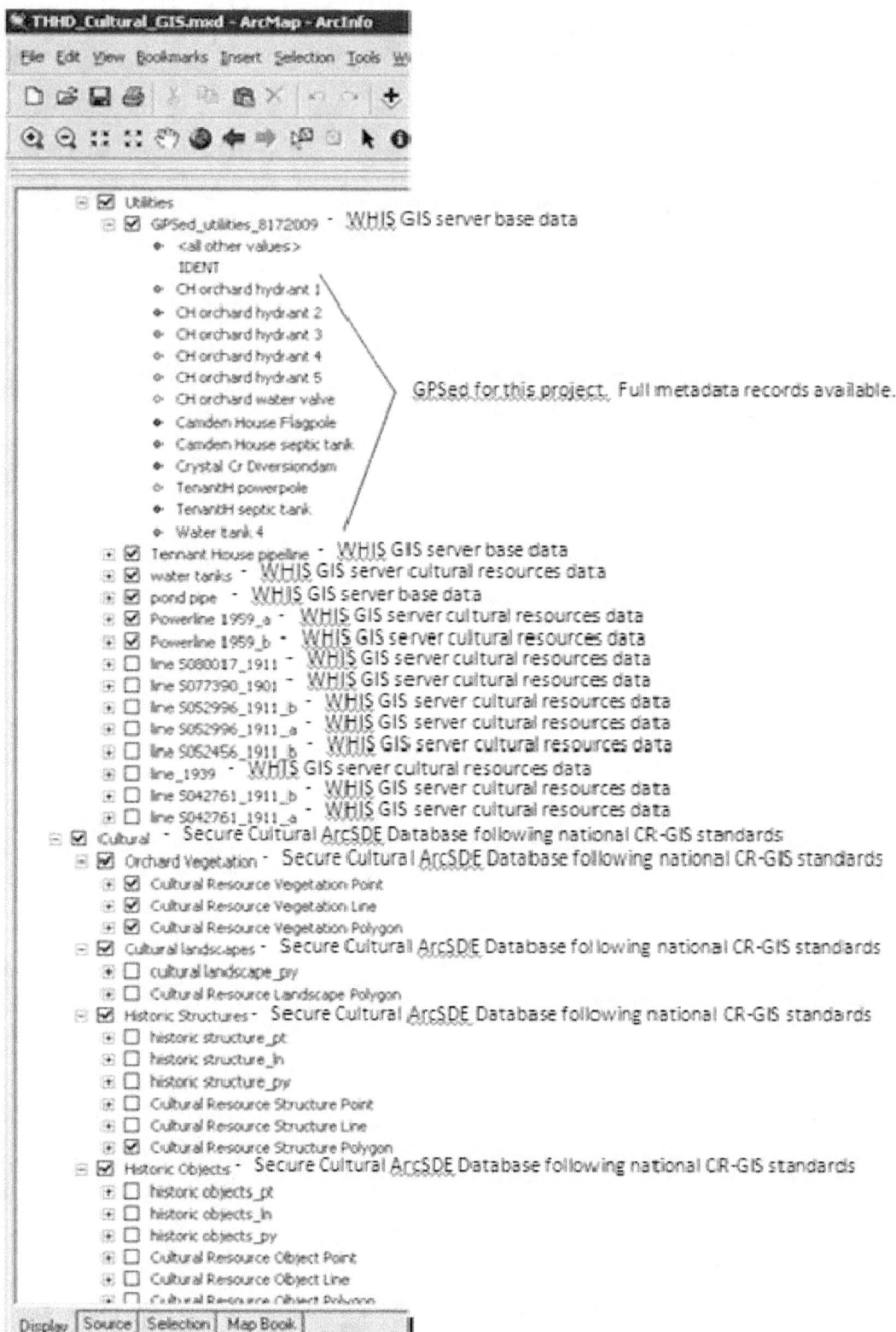

THHD_Cultural_GIS.mxd - ArcMap - ArcInfo

File Edit View Bookmarks Insert Selection Tools W

☐ ☑ Utilities
   ☐ ☑ GPSed_utilities_8172009 - WHIS GIS server base data
     ◆ <all other values>
      IDENT
     ◆ CH orchard hydrant 1
     ◆ CH orchard hydrant 2
     ◆ CH orchard hydrant 3
     ◆ CH orchard hydrant 4
     ◆ CH orchard hydrant 5
     ◇ CH orchard water valve   GPSed for this project. Full metadata records available.
     ◆ Camden House Flagpole
     ◆ Camden House septic tank
     ◆ Crystal Cr Diversiondam
     ◇ TenantH powerpole
     ◆ TenantH septic tank
     ◆ Water tank 4
  ☐ ☑ Tennant House pipeline - WHIS GIS server base data
  ☐ ☑ water tanks - WHIS GIS server cultural resources data
  ☐ ☑ pond pipe - WHIS GIS server base data
  ☐ ☑ Powerline 1959_a - WHIS GIS server cultural resources data
  ☐ ☑ Powerline 1959_b - WHIS GIS server cultural resources data
  ☐ ☐ line S080017_1911 - WHIS GIS server cultural resources data
  ☐ ☐ line S077390_1901 - WHIS GIS server cultural resources data
  ☐ ☐ line S052996_1911_b - WHIS GIS server cultural resources data
  ☐ ☐ line S052996_1911_a - WHIS GIS server cultural resources data
  ☐ ☐ line S052456_1911_b - WHIS GIS server cultural resources data
  ☐ ☐ line_1939 - WHIS GIS server cultural resources data
  ☐ ☐ line S042761_1911_b - WHIS GIS server cultural resources data
  ☐ ☐ line S042761_1911_a - WHIS GIS server cultural resources data
☐ ☑ Cultural - Secure Cultural ArcSDE Database following national CR-GIS standards
  ☐ ☑ Orchard Vegetation - Secure Cultural ArcSDE Database following national CR-GIS standards
    ☐ ☑ Cultural Resource Vegetation Point
    ☐ ☑ Cultural Resource Vegetation Line
    ☐ ☑ Cultural Resource Vegetation Polygon
  ☐ ☑ Cultural landscapes - Secure Cultural ArcSDE Database following national CR-GIS standards
    ☐ ☐ cultural landscape_py
    ☐ ☐ Cultural Resource Landscape Polygon
  ☐ ☑ Historic Structures - Secure Cultural ArcSDE Database following national CR-GIS standards
    ☐ ☐ historic structure_pt
    ☐ ☐ historic structure_ln
    ☐ ☐ historic structure_py
    ☐ ☐ Cultural Resource Structure Point
    ☐ ☐ Cultural Resource Structure Line
    ☐ ☑ Cultural Resource Structure Polygon
  ☐ ☑ Historic Objects - Secure Cultural ArcSDE Database following national CR-GIS standards
    ☐ ☐ historic objects_pt
    ☐ ☐ historic objects_ln
    ☐ ☐ historic objects_py
    ☐ ☐ Cultural Resource Object Point
    ☐ ☐ Cultural Resource Object Line
    ☐ ☐ Cultural Resource Object Polygon

Display | Source | Selection | Map Book

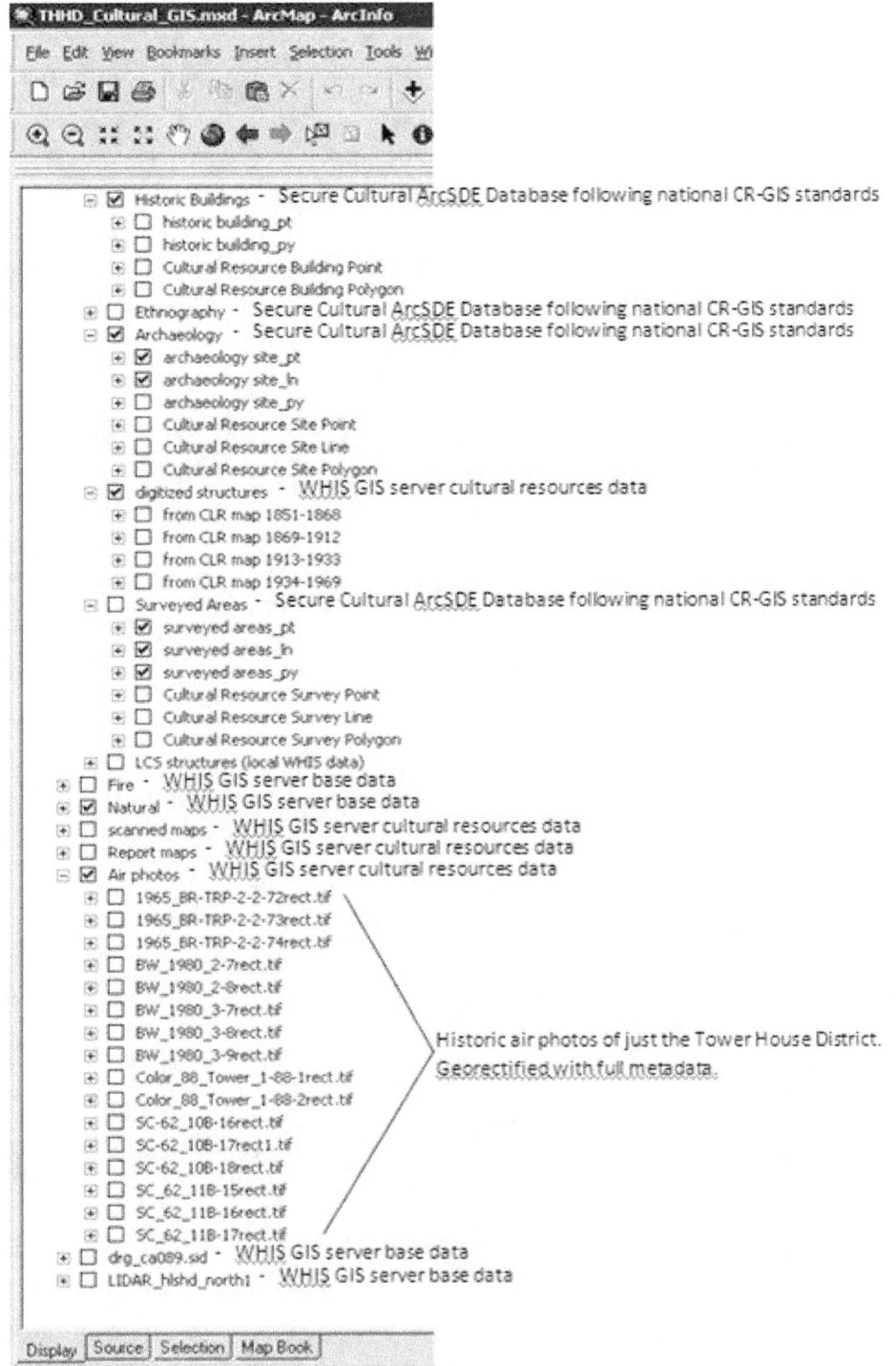

THHD_Cultural_GIS.mxd - ArcMap - ArcInfo

File Edit View Bookmarks Insert Selection Tools W

☑ Historic Buildings - Secure Cultural ArcSDE Database following national CR-GIS standards
  ☐ historic building_pt
  ☐ historic building_py
  ☐ Cultural Resource Building Point
  ☐ Cultural Resource Building Polygon
☐ Ethnography - Secure Cultural ArcSDE Database following national CR-GIS standards
☑ Archaeology - Secure Cultural ArcSDE Database following national CR-GIS standards
  ☑ archaeology site_pt
  ☑ archaeology site_ln
  ☐ archaeology site_py
  ☐ Cultural Resource Site Point
  ☐ Cultural Resource Site Line
  ☐ Cultural Resource Site Polygon
☑ digitized structures - WHIS GIS server cultural resources data
  ☐ from CLR map 1851-1868
  ☐ from CLR map 1869-1912
  ☐ from CLR map 1913-1933
  ☐ from CLR map 1934-1969
☐ Surveyed Areas - Secure Cultural ArcSDE Database following national CR-GIS standards
  ☑ surveyed areas_pt
  ☑ surveyed areas_ln
  ☑ surveyed areas_py
  ☐ Cultural Resource Survey Point
  ☐ Cultural Resource Survey Line
  ☐ Cultural Resource Survey Polygon
☐ LCS structures (local WHIS data)
☐ Fire - WHIS GIS server base data
☑ Natural - WHIS GIS server base data
☐ scanned maps - WHIS GIS server cultural resources data
☐ Report maps - WHIS GIS server cultural resources data
☑ Air photos - WHIS GIS server cultural resources data
  ☐ 1965_BR-TRP-2-2-72rect.tif
  ☐ 1965_BR-TRP-2-2-73rect.tif
  ☐ 1965_BR-TRP-2-2-74rect.tif
  ☐ BW_1980_2-7rect.tif
  ☐ BW_1980_2-8rect.tif
  ☐ BW_1980_3-7rect.tif
  ☐ BW_1980_3-8rect.tif
  ☐ BW_1980_3-9rect.tif
  ☐ Color_88_Tower_1-88-1rect.tif
  ☐ Color_88_Tower_1-88-2rect.tif
  ☐ SC-62_10B-16rect.tif
  ☐ SC-62_10B-17rect1.tif
  ☐ SC-62_10B-18rect.tif
  ☐ SC_62_11B-15rect.tif
  ☐ SC_62_11B-16rect.tif
  ☐ SC_62_11B-17rect.tif
☐ drg_ca089.sid - WHIS GIS server base data
☐ LIDAR_hlshd_north1 - WHIS GIS server base data

Historic air photos of just the Tower House District. Georectified with full metadata.

Display | Source | Selection | Map Book

23

Appendix C: Cultural Resources GIS Data Standards

Sponsor(s): John J. Knoerl (NPS Cultural Resource GIS Facility)
Data Steward(s): John J. Knoerl NPS Cultural Resource GIS Facility
Data Contact(s): Deidre McCarthy

Layer Status: Review Draft
Status Date: 07/31/2009

NPS Cultural Resource Data Exchange Standard Review Draft

Background: The NPS Cultural Resources Data Transfer Standard - Geometry is a series of data transfer standards for cultural resources. The series is composed of data transfer standards for NPS Historic District Polygon Data Transfer Standard, NPS Historic Landscape Polygon Data Transfer Standard, NPS Historic Building Polygon Data Transfer Standard, NPS Historic Building Point Data Transfer Standard, NPS Historic Structure Polygon Data Transfer Standard, NPS Historic Structure Line Data Transfer Standard, NPS Historic Structure Point Data Transfer Standard, NPS Archeological Site Polygon Data Transfer Standard, NPS Archaeological Site Line Data Transfer Standard, NPS Archeological Site Point Data Transfer Standard, and NPS Historic Object Point Data Transfer Standard. For purposes of these standards the term Historic refers to cultural resources which could be historic, prehistoric, or ethnographic.

Abstract: This review draft data transfer standard describes a proposed structure for archeological sites, historic sites, historic districts, historic landscapes, historic objects, and historic structures depicted as lines, points, or polygons. Multiple feature geometries may coexist for the same archeological site as a result of overlapping surveys each with their own particular purpose and bias. All archeological sites identified on cultural resource inventories of Federal agencies including the National Park Service, and optionally, State and Tribal Historic Preservation Offices, are covered by this data transfer standard. Attribute data are intentionally limited to those necessary for spatial data maintenance and feature level metadata. Data from external database systems are intended to link with these data to provide basic feature attributes. The means to maintain unique identifiers for each archeological site (CR_ID), Survey_ID, as well as unique geometries associated with that feature (GIS_LOC_ID) are through the use of Globally Unique Identifiers (GUIDs) assigned by the database. Information about the source and vintage of individual polygons are documented within the Edit_Date and CR_Notes attributes.

Purpose: A current, accurate representation of all inventoried cultural resources is of interest to Federal agencies, the NPS, and its State and Tribal preservation partners. This interest stems from the regulatory processes of managing cultural resources that are consistent with the National Historic Preservation Act as Amended, the National Environmental Policy Act as Amended, the Archaeological Resources Protection Act, and other laws related to cultural resources. The regulations promulgating these laws require the use of spatial data in support of various decisions and actions related to cultural resource management. Cultural resource geospatial information is also needed by NPS personnel, cooperators, and the public for map display and analysis. Collectively, the cultural resource datasets are intended to be a comprehensive inventory of all cultural resources of interest to the Federal government. This dataset provides feature geometry and is intended to be supplemented with attributes maintained by other external database systems.

GIS DATA STANDARD: This is a review draft of a proposed NPS GIS data transfer standard. This standard is sponsored by the NPS GIS Cultural Resource Facility, the NPS GIS Committee in cooperation with the GISD. The data steward shall be the Cultural Resources GIS Facility through the coordinated contributions of many programs.

DATA MODEL: This data standard is designed to accomodate base cartographic requirements and the systematic inventory of all NPS Heritage Assets. The main premise of the data standards is to keep the attribute structure as minimal as possible, enforce database normalization, eliminate redundant data, and support the base mapping requirements of the NPS and its partners. The specific model that will be implemented is not proposed in this standard. It is anticipated that both enterprise and disconnected park-based implementations will be necessary. The models shall be designed after approval of the data transfer standard.

Positional accuracy:
Horizontal positional accuracy:
    Horizontal positional accuracy report: Minimum standard of 1:24,000 National Map Accuracy Standards (NMAS). Equivalent to a maximum horizontal positional error of 40 feet for 90% of all well-defined points. Accuracy is desired at 1:12,000 NMAS or better if attainable.
Point and vector object information:
    SDTS terms description:
    Name: CR_data
    SDTS point and vector object type: G-polygon
    Point and vector object count: 0
Spatial Reference Information:
    Horizontal coordinate system definition:
    Coordinate system name:
    Geographic coordinate system name: GCS_North_American_1983

Geographic:
Latitude resolution: 0.0000001
Longitude resolution: 0.0000001
Geographic coordinate units: Decimal degrees

Geodetic model:
Horizontal datum name: North American Datum of 1983
Ellipsoid name: Geodetic Reference System 80
Semi-major axis: 6378137.000000
Denominator of flattening ratio: 298.257222

Link to Data File(s) (Network Resource Name):
http://nrdata.nps.gov/gisc/data_standards/reviewdraft.zip

Attributes of nps_hist_district_poly *Type of object (entity type): Feature Class*

Attribute Name	Long Attribute Name	Data Type	Width	Value: Definition	Description	Domain Values	Values: Formal Codeset
OBJECTID	OBJECTID	OID	4	MANDATORY: Internal feature number. (*Source:* ESRI)	Sequential unique whole numbers that are automatically generated.		
SHAPE	SHAPE	Geometry	0	MANDATORY: Specifies the geometry of the feature (*Source:* ESRI)	Coordinates defining the features		
LENGTH	SHAPE_LENGTH	Double	8	MANDATORY IF APPLICABLE: Length of feature in internal units. (*Source:* ESRI)	Positive real numbers that are automatically generated.		
CR_ID	NPS_CULTURAL_RESOURCE_ID, CULTURAL_RESOURCE_ID	String	128	MANDATORY: Unique identifier of the cultural resource. (*Source:* NPS Cultural Resource GIS Facility)	A GUID (Globally Unique IDentifier) is a 128 bit number that can be expressed in string format and is a standard method in MS Windows of generating an identifier virtually guaranteed to be unique regardless of its source. GUID's allow systems/users to generate their own identifiers with near certainty that they will be Globally Unique. Automated tools for generating GUID's will be included in the implementation template.		
SURVEY_ID	NPS_CULTURAL_RESOURCE_SURVEY_ID, CULTURAL_RESOURCE_ID	String	128	MANDATORY: Unique identifier of the survey in which the cultural resource is associated. (*Source:* NPS Cultural Resource GIS Facility)	A GUID (Globally Unique IDentifier) is a 128 bit number that can be expressed in string format and is a standard method in MS Windows of generating an identifier virtually guaranteed to be unique regardless of its source. GUID's allow systems/users to generate their own identifiers with near certainty that they will be Globally Unique. Automated tools for generating GUID's will be included in the implementation template.		

28

Attributes of nps_hist_district_poly *Type of object (entity type)*: **Feature Class**

Attribute Name	Long Attribute Name	Data Type	Width	Value: Definition	Description	Domain Values	Values: Formal Codeset
GIS_LOC_ID	NPS_LOC ATION_ID ; LOCATIO N_ID	String	128	MANDATORY: Unique identifier of the feature geometry type. (*Source:* Data specifications for Resource Mapping, Inventories, and Studies - NPS Natural Resource Program Center)	A GUID (Globally Unique IDentifier) is a 128 bit number that can be expressed in string format and is a standard method in MS Windows of generating an identifier virtually guaranteed to be unique regardless of its source. GUID's allow systems/users to generate their own identifiers with near certainty that they will be Globally Unique. Automated tools for generating GUID's will be included in the implementation template.		
BND_TYPE	NPS_CUL TURAL_R ESOURC E_BOUN DARY_TY PE, CULTUR AL_RESO URCE_B OUNDAR Y_TYPE	String	3	MANDATORY: Code describing the type of boundary drawn to represent the cultural resource. (*Source:* NPS Cultural Resource GIS Facility)		NPS_CULTURAL_RE SOURCE_BOUNDAR Y_TYPE, CULTURAL_RESOU RCE_BOUNDARY_T YPE:	Codeset Name: Codes describin g the type of boundary. Codeset Source: NPS Cultural Resource GIS Facility

Attributes of nps_hist_district_poly *Type of object (entity type):* **Feature Class**

Attribute Name	Long Attribute Name	Data Type	Width	Value: Definition	Description	Domain Values	Values: Formal Codeset
IS_EXTANT	NPS_IS_EXTANT, IS_EXTANT	String	7	MANDATORY: Code describing whether the cultural resource is extant. (*Source:* NPS Cultural Resource GIS Facility)			Codeset Name: Codes describing whether the cultural resource is extant.
						NPS_IS_EXTANT, IS_EXTANT:	Codeset Source: NPS Cultural Resource GIS Facility
RESTRICT	NPS_CR_RESTRICT_STATUS, CR_RESTRICT_ST ATUS	String	3	MANDATORY: Code describing the type of restriction on release of locational data. (*Source:* NPS Cultural Resource GIS Facility)			Codeset Name: Codes describing the type of restriction on release of locational data
						NPS_CR_RESTRICT_STATUS, CR_RESTRICT_STA TUS:	Codeset Source: NPS Cultural Resource GIS Facility

30

Attributes of nps_hist_district_poly *Type of object (entity type)*: **Feature Class**

Attribute Name	Long Attribute Name	Data Type	Width	Value: Definition	Description	Domain Values	Values: Formal Codeset
SOURCE	NPS_SOURCE, SOURCE	String	255	MANDATORY: Source name and institutional affiliation responsible for creating the source spatial document. (*Source:* NPS Cultural Resource GIS Facility)	Free text (up to 255 characters)		
SRC_DATE	NPS_SOURCE_DATE, SOURCE_DATE	String	8	MANDATORY: Date the feature was created by the source (*Source:* NPS Cultural Resource GIS Facility)	Valid date entered in YYYYMMDD format		
SRC_SCALE	NPS_SOURCE_SCALE, SOURCE_SCALE	String	20	MANDATORY: Original scale at which the feature was mapped. (*Source:* NPS Cultural Resource GIS Facility)	---		
SRC_ACCU	NPS_SOURCE_ACCURACY, SOURCE_ACCURACY	String	255	MANDATORY: Statement describing the accuracy of the data.	Free text (up to 255 characters)		

31

Attributes of nps_hist_district_poly *Type of object (entity type):* **Feature Class**

Attribute Name	Long Attribute Name	Data Type	Width	Value: Definition	Description	Domain Values	Values: Formal Codeset
SRC_COORD	NPS_SO URCE_C OORD_S YS, SOURCE _COORD _SYS	String	50	MANDATORY: Code describing the original coordinate system at which the feature was mapped. (*Source:* NPS Cultural Resource GIS Facility)		NPS_SOURCE_COO RD_SYS, SOURCE_COORD_S YS:	
MAP_METHOD	NPS_MA P_METH OD, MAP_ME THOD	String	4	MANDATORY: Code describing how spatial data was collected or captured (*Source:* NPS GIS-Commitee)			Codeset Name: Codes defining how data were collected
						NPS_MAP_METHOD, MAP_METHOD:	Codeset Source: NPS
EDIT_DATE	NPS_EDI T_DATE, EDIT_DA TE	String	8	MANDATORY: The last edit, update, or official review of the GIS/location record. (*Source:* NPS GIS-Committee)	Valid date entered in YYYYMMDD format		

Attributes of nps_hist_district_poly *Type of object (entity type):* **Feature Class**

Attribute Name	Long Attribute Name	Data Type	Width	Value: Definition	Description	Domain Values	Values: Formal Codeset
CR_NOTES	NPS_CUL TURAL_R ESOURC E_NOTES ; CULTUR AL_RESO URCE_N OTES	String	255	OPTIONAL: Notes or remarks needed to understand unusual aspects of the spatial data. (*Source:* NPS Cultural Resource GIS Facility)	Free text (up to 255 characters)		
CONSTRAINT	NPS_CR_ DATA_C ONSTRAI NTS, CR_DATA _CONST RAINTS	String	255	OPTIONAL: Notes or remarks needed to convey the appropriate use of the spatial data. (*Source:* NPS Cultural Resource GIS Facility)	Free text (up to 255 characters)		

NPS GIS Layer Standards stylesheet modified from FGDC Classic and DataDictionTable stylesheets provided courtesy of ESRI.

Appendix D: Statement of Procedures

SOP Table of Contents

Remote Desktop

In order to access the Tower House Historical GIS project, you will first need to remote desktop into the server. Navigate through the start menu to find the Remote Desktop Connection application. It is usually found in the Accessories folder in All Programs through the Start menu.

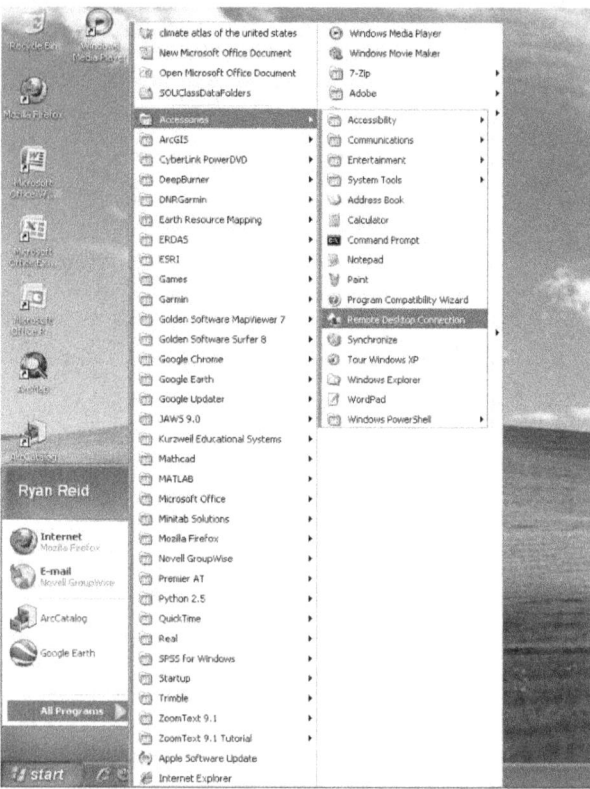

Click on the Remote Desktop Connection application and a dialog box appears on the screen.

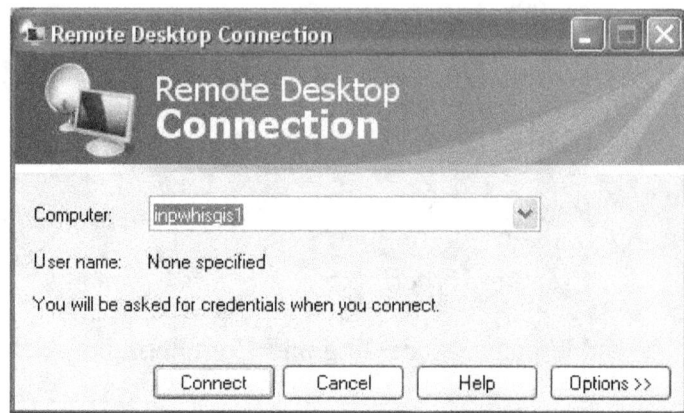

In the empty box next to the label "Computer:" type **inpwhisgis1**. Click connect, and a second dialog box will appear asking for your username and password. Enter both and select NPS from the dropdown menu. Click OK. Now you have remotely accessed the server.

Locating the ArcMap project

Once you have connected to the server you can now locate and access the ArcMap document. Follow this path: **N:\GIS_Projects\02_ARCH_TowerhouseGIS\Final**.

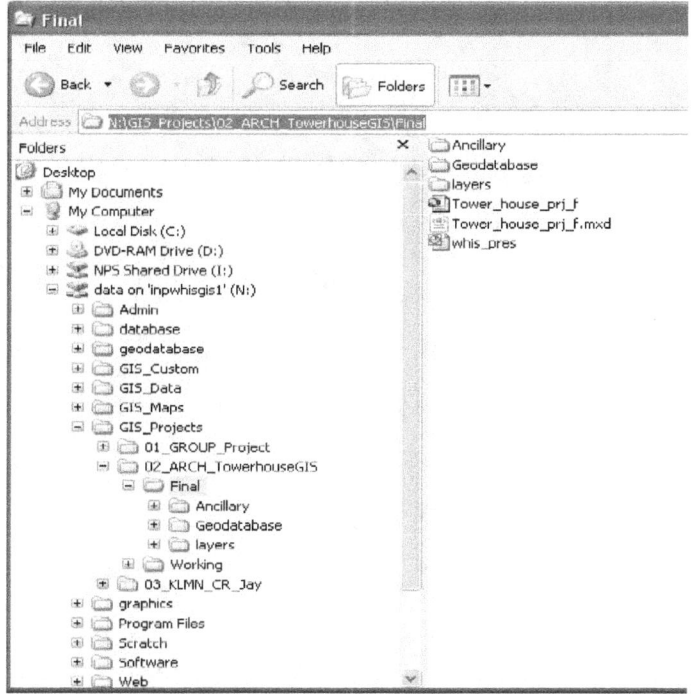

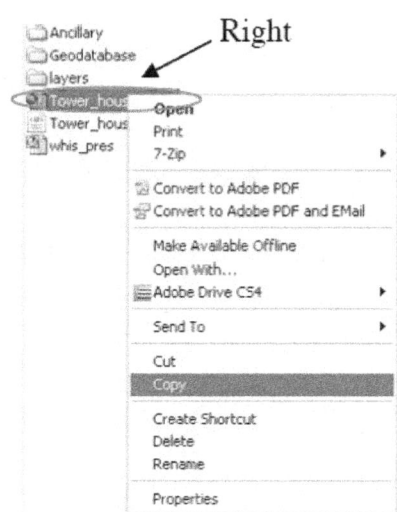

STOP!(PLEASE READ): Before opening the **THHD_Cultural_GIS** ArcMap document, **RIGHT CLICK** on the file and **COPY** the file to your own computer or own location on the server.

If you do not copy the file to your own computer or own location on the server, you will not be able to make changes to the ArcMap document. To have full control of the file, to add or remove layers, you must copy the file to your own computer or own location on the server.

Adding Data

To add data, click the "add data" ✛ button on the horizontal toolbar above the main window. Navigate through the folders to find the data that you wish to enter. Select the data and click "add".

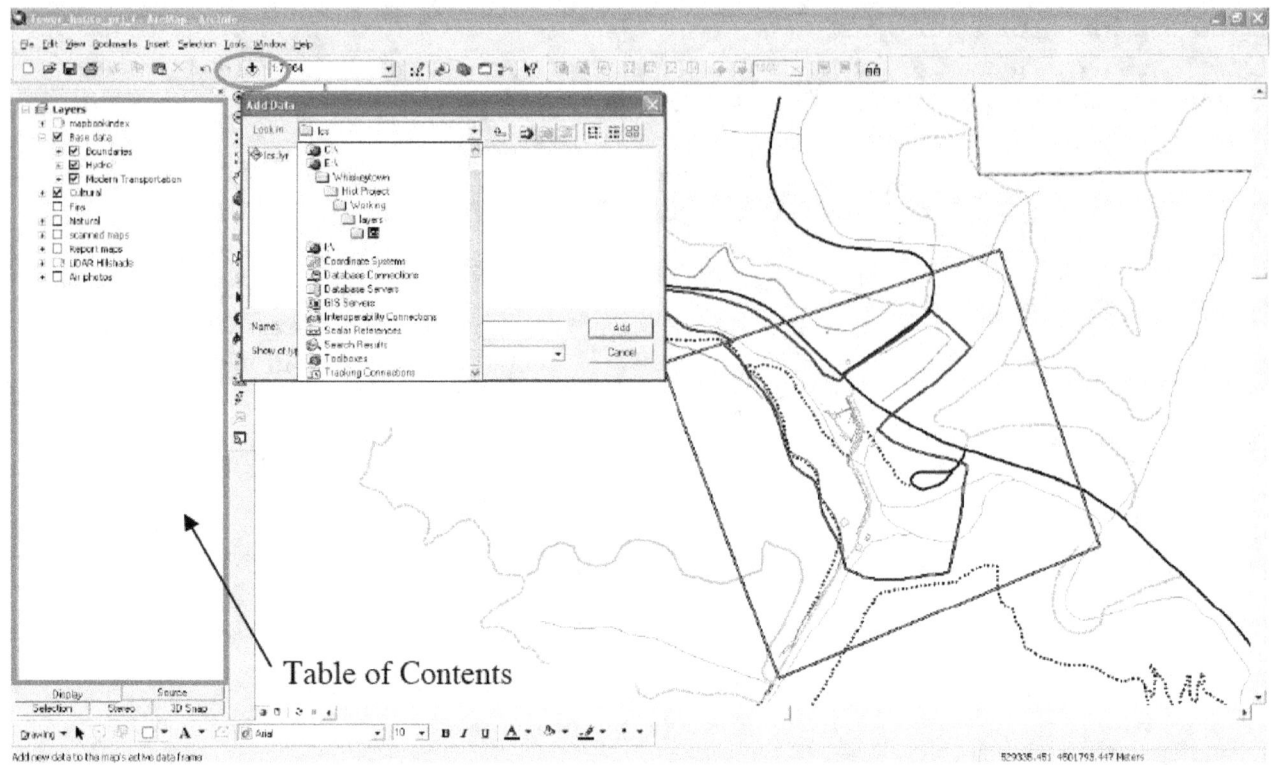

Table of Contents

The data you have just entered will display as the first layer in the table of contents. Layers that are at the top of the list in the table of contents will be displayed on top of other layers on the map (so if you have an aerial photo at the top of the list of layers, everything else will be buried underneath it on the map). You can move the layer up or down the table of contents by clicking and holding the mouse button on the layer you want to move, then dragging the layer to its destination and releasing the mouse button.

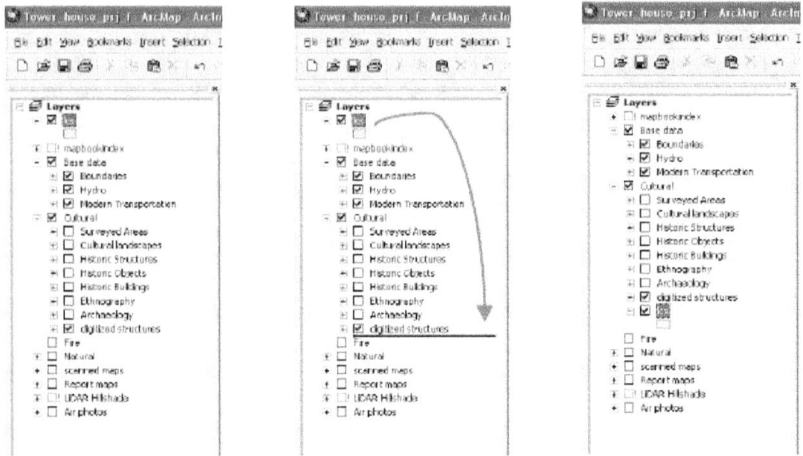

Removing Data
To remove data, right click on the layer you wish to remove and click on "remove" in the pop up menu.

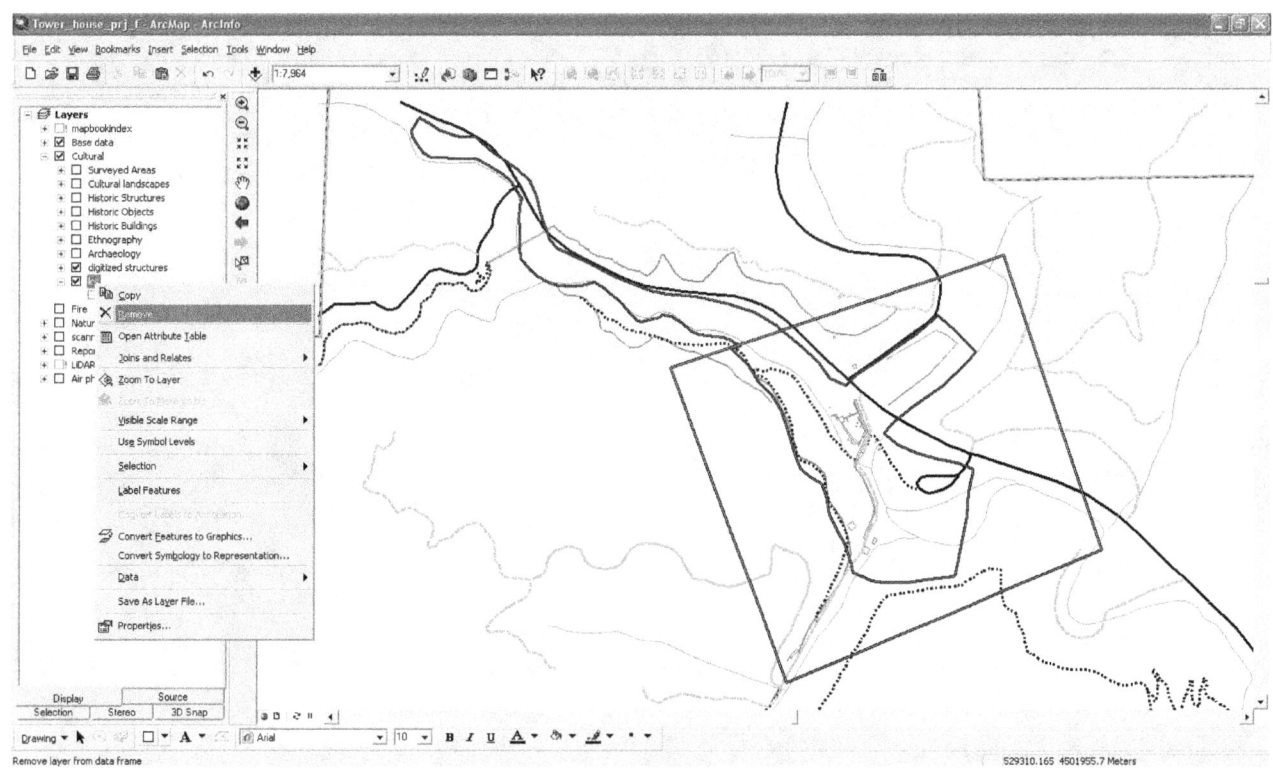

Creating Hyperlinks

Hyperlinks are used to link any ancillary data (photos, .pdf etc.) to data in the ArcMap document.

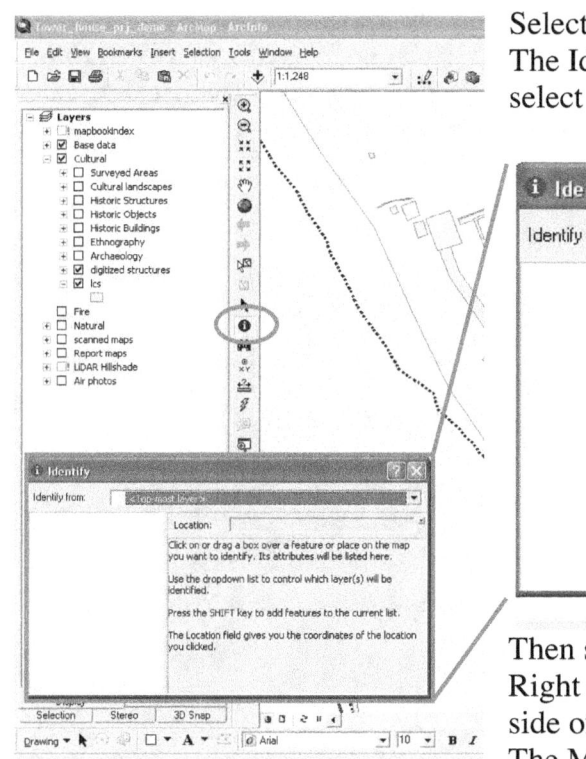

Select the Identifier Tool, ⓘ on the navigation toolbar. The Identify window will open. In the drop down menu select the layer you wish to indentify features from.

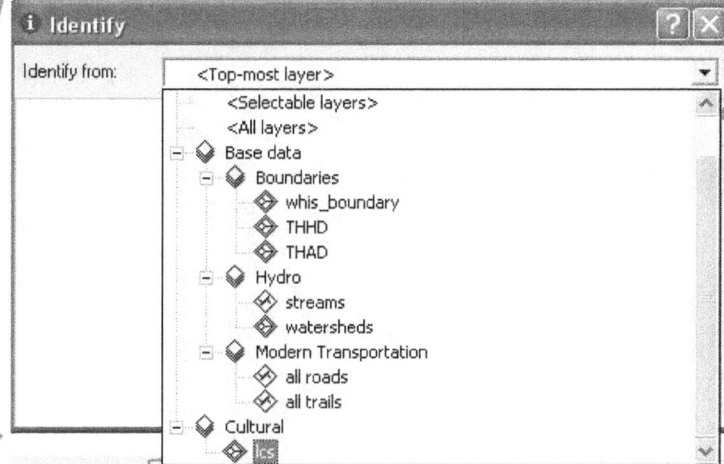

Then select the feature you wish to add a hyperlink to. Right click on the name of the feature in the tree on the left side of the Identify window. Click on **Manage Hyperlinks**. The Manage Dynamic Hyperlinks window will appear.

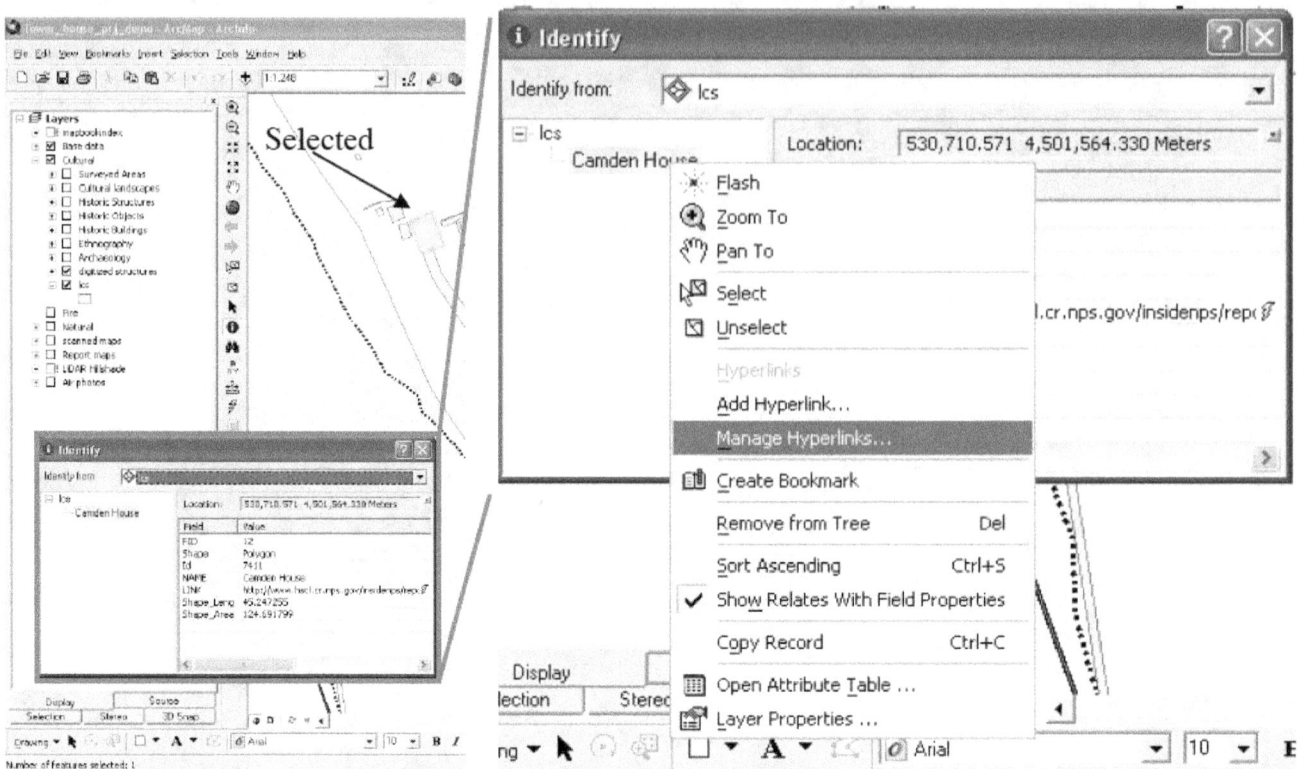

In the Manage Dynamic Hyperlinks window, click on **Add New** and the Add Hyperlink window will appear. In the Add Hyperlink window you have the option to link to either a document (including photos) or a URL. Select which you wish to link to. If you wish to link to a URL, type the complete URL in the box provided under the label. If you wish to link to a document (including photos) click the browse button, a window titled "Open" will appear and allow you to choose which document to attach.

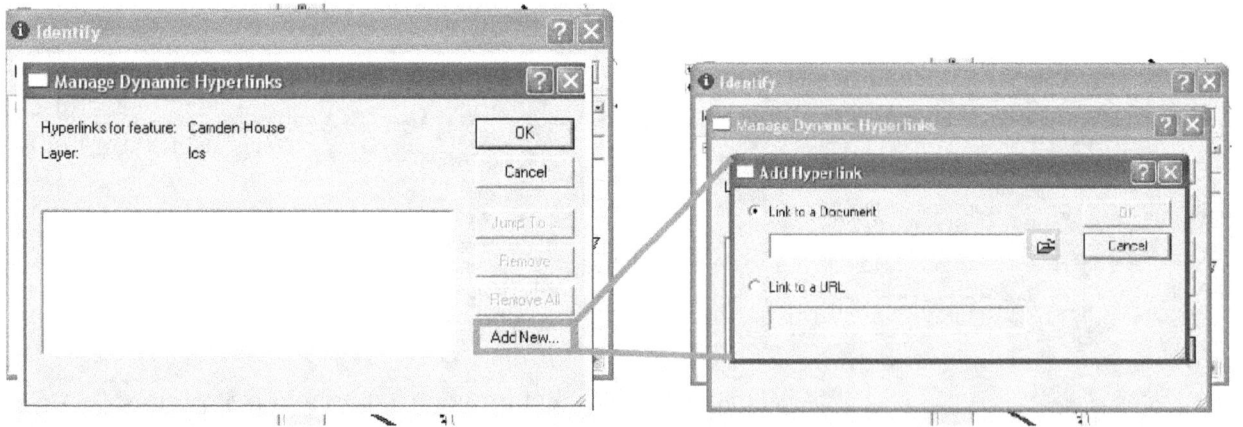

Navigate through the folders to the location of the document or photo you wish to link, select the document or photo and click Open. The path of the document or photo you selected to link will show in the box under the "Link to a Document" label. Click OK to add a hyperlink to the selected document.

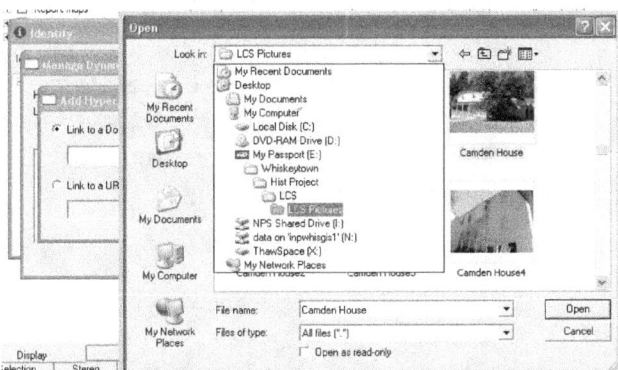
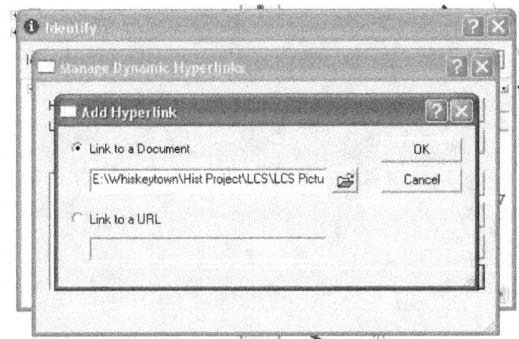

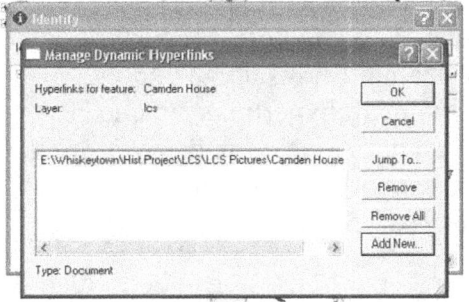

When the Add Hyperlink window closes, the document or photo will show as a link in the Manage Dynamic Hyperlinks window. If you are satisfied with the link you have just created, click OK. If not, you can remove the link by clicking Remove. If you wish to link to more than one document or a URL, click Add New and follow the same steps.

If you wish to remove a link when there is more than one showing in the Manage Dynamic Hyperlinks window, be sure to select (by clicking on the link) the link you wish to remove, then click Remove. If you want to remove all links, click Remove All.

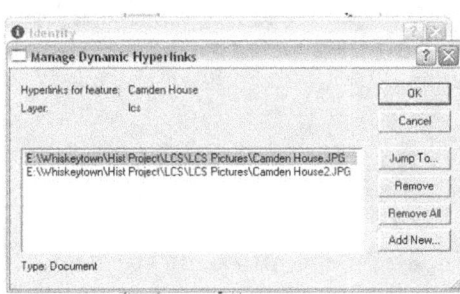

Click OK when you have finished linking and you will be taken back to the ArcMap document. You may close the Identify window if you choose.

To view the links you have created in the ArcMap document, select the Hyperlink Tool. The mouse cursor will change to a lightning bolt and the features in the ArcMap document that have links will change to blue signifying that they have hyperlinks. If the feature you linked to is a point, the point will turn blue. If the feature is a polygon, the polygon outline will turn blue. And if the feature is a line, the line will turn blue.

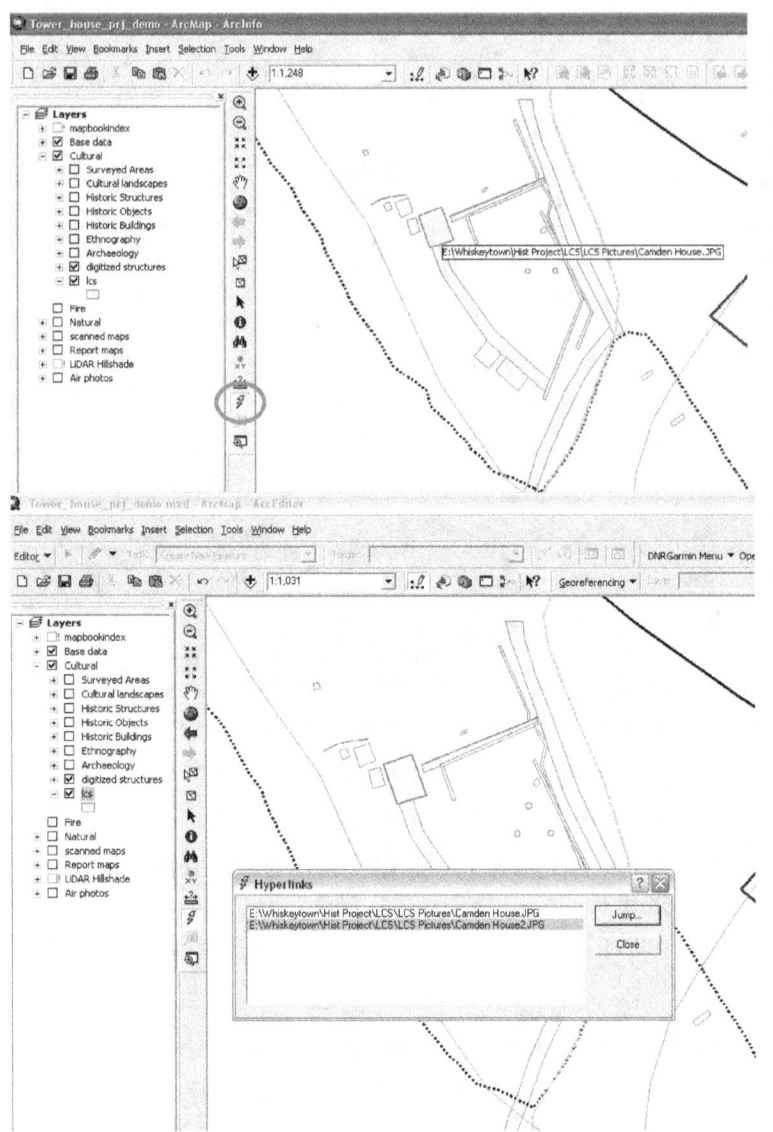

Hover the cursor over the linked feature and the lightning bolt will change to black, also signifying that the feature has a hyperlink. A box will popup displaying the path of the linked document, photo or URL. Click on the linked feature and your link will open.

When two or more hyperlinks are attached to a feature, clicking on the feature brings up a window showing all hyperlinks attached to the feature. Select the link you wish to view and click Jump. Only the link you select will open.

Metadata: Accessing and Completing

To access metadata, in **ArcCatalog** navigate through the folder tree to the location of the data you wish to complete metadata for. Highlight the data by clicking once on the name of the file. Then select the Metadata Tab to view any metadata that the data may have.

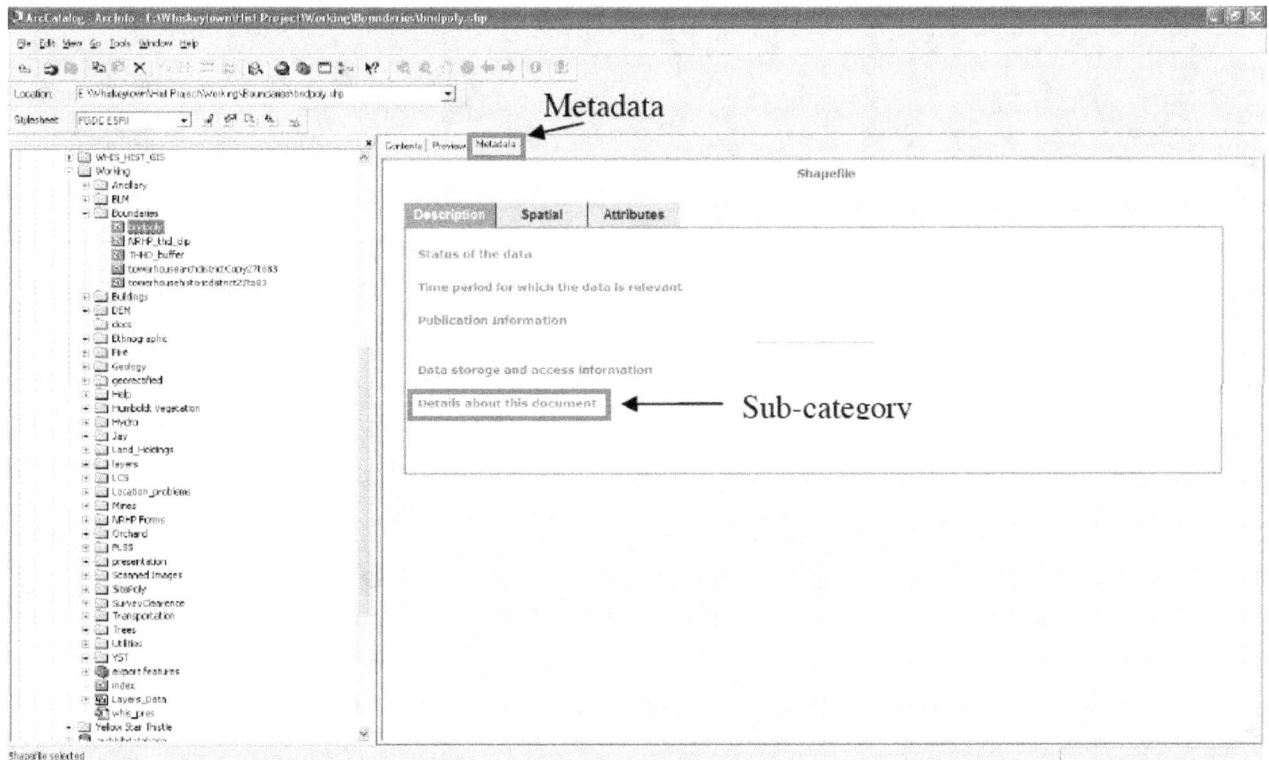

Metadata

Sub-category

To view metadata associated with the data, click on the green sub-category headings. Metadata relevant to each sub-category will appear below the headings. Click the green heading a second time to hide the metadata.

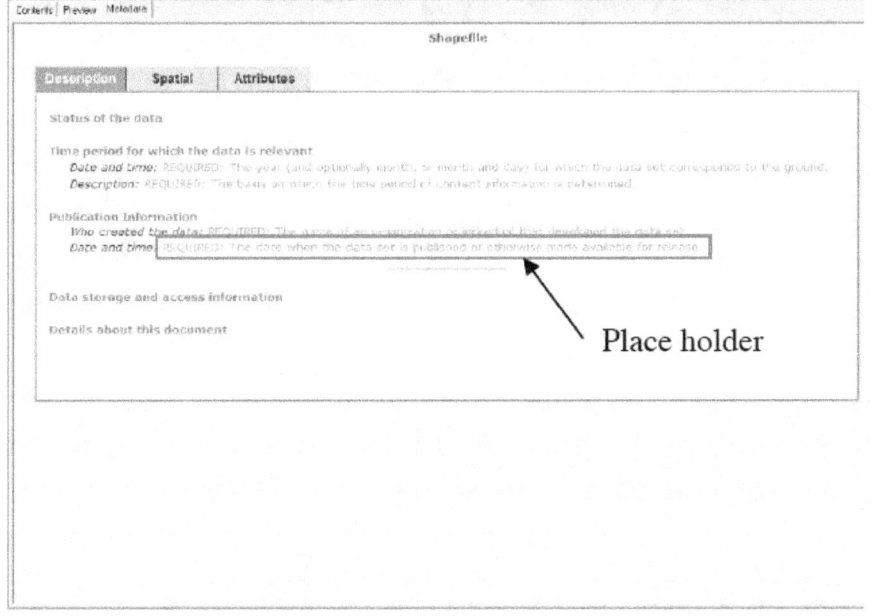

Place holder

If the sub-categories do not contain any metadata there is usually a place holder text in the field that requires metadata. Metadata in sub-categories with green headings needs to be entered manually.

To view different aspects of the metadata click a different descriptive tab within the metadata. Additional metadata will appear.

Blue sub-category headings mean that metadata relevant to that sub-category updates on the fly. Ex: If you were to change the projection of this particular shapefile, the metadata will update the projection to whatever you changed it to. These subcategories do not need any metadata completion.

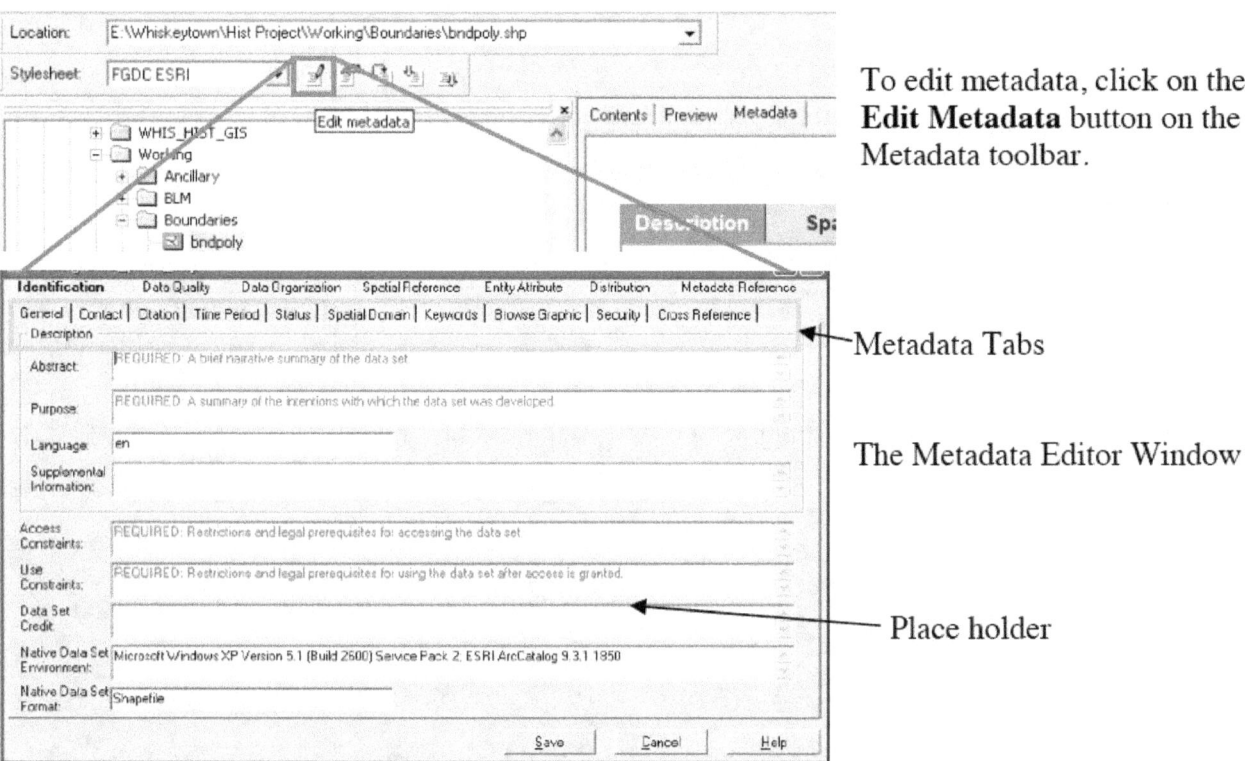

To edit metadata, click on the **Edit Metadata** button on the Metadata toolbar.

Metadata Tabs

The Metadata Editor Window

Place holder

There are many tabs within the metadata editor. Go through the tabs and add as much information about the data as possible. The more information entered, the more a user will know about the origin of the data. There may be some fields that you might not know what to enter. At least, complete all of the required fields so other users can have an idea of what the data are referring to.

To enter text into a field, highlight the red place holder text, press either the Delete or Backspace key and then you can enter whatever text you wish.

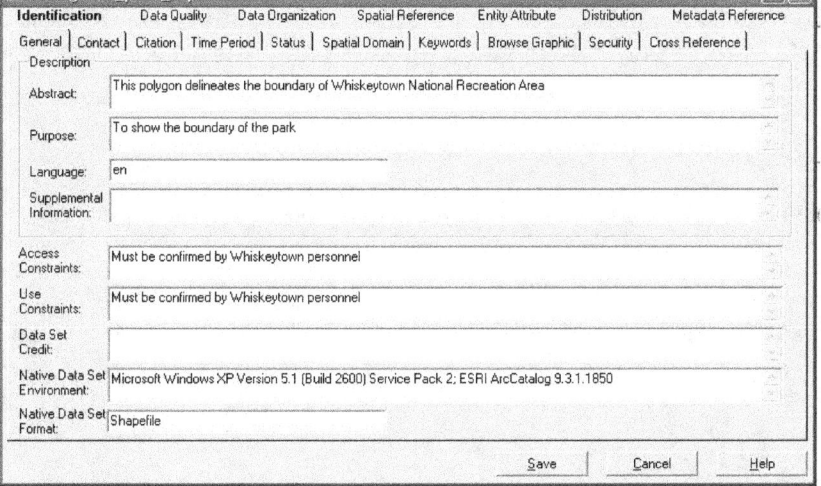

After entering information into the desired fields, click Save and you will be taken back to the Metadata view. The information you have entered will appear in the sub-categories to which the information is relevant.

To save time, you can create a metadata template with basic information such as keywords and contact details to import to the metadata. To create a template, view metadata for a data file, add any basic information that will be used for all data files and remove information that is not general in nature. If the file you opened contains specific information to that file such an abstract, purpose, and a title, it needs to be removed. Or to save what is in the field, copy it to any word processing program to reuse later. Click Save when you are satisfied with the basic information you have entered. Then click the Export Metadata button found on the same toolbar as the Edit Metadata button.

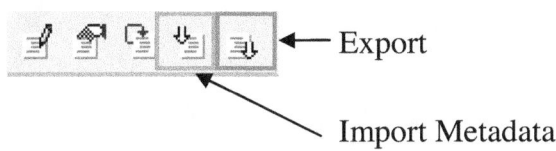

Note: If you leave a title in the template you are creating, the title will be a part of the template. That title will appear as the title for every file you import the template to.

45

By clicking the Export Metadata button the Export Metadata window will appear. Select which format to save your template as from the drop down menu. Then click Browse to choose the location to save the template to. Give the file a name, i.e. template, then click Save. The browse window will close and then click OK in the Export Metadata window. You have now successfully created a metadata template.

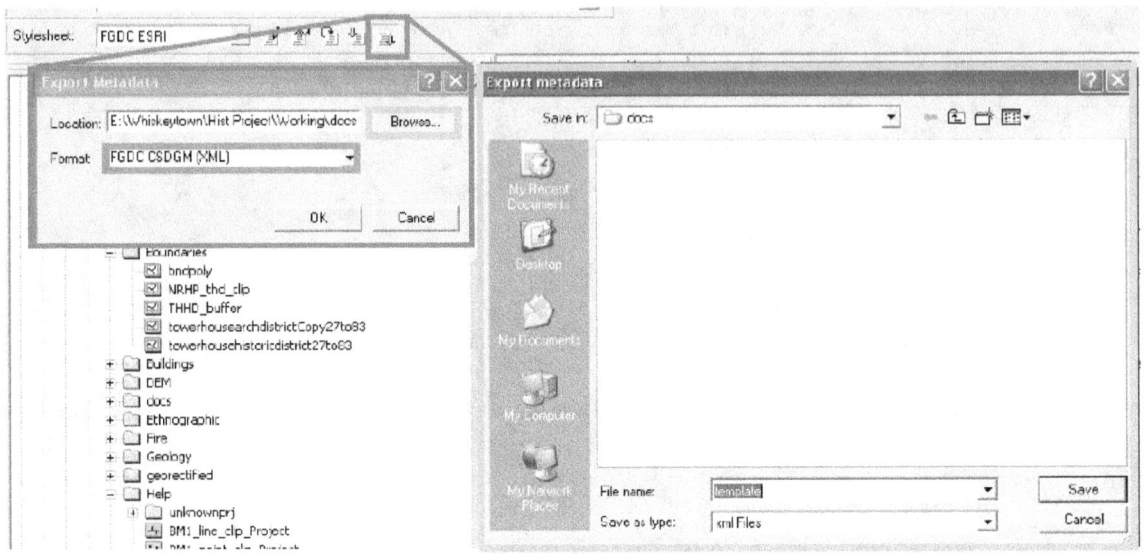

To import metadata, select the file you wish to import to, click the metadata tab, then click the Import Metadata button on the Metadata toolbar and the Import Metadata window will appear. Select the proper format of which you saved your template as from the drop down menu. Then click Browse and navigate to the location of your saved template, select the file and click Open. The browse window will close and then click OK in the Import Metadata window. Your metadata template has now been successfully imported.

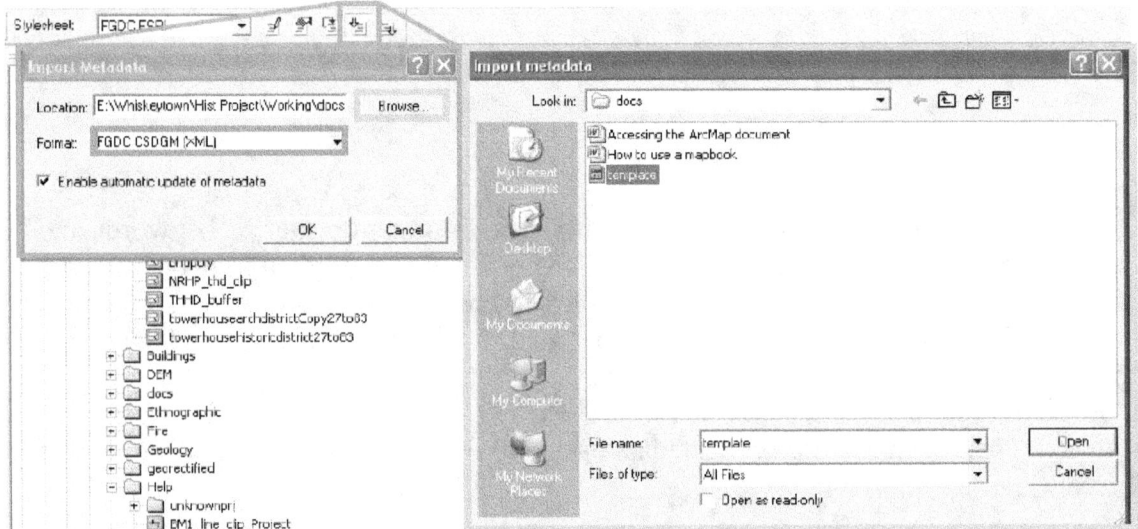

Creating Layers

Creating layer files from shapefiles allows the user to edit the file's properties and save them. **Editing the layer properties does not change the source feature class.** If you open the properties of a shapefile using ArcCatalog, you will find only certain aspects can be changed. But if you create a layer from that shapefile, then open layer properties, more aspects become editable. Since feature symbology cannot be saved to a shapefile, ArcMap gives the shapefile a default color once added to the ArcMap document. If you decide to change the symbology of a layer through the layer properties in ArcCatalog, the layer, when added to an ArcMap document, will always have the symbology you chose to give it.

Shapefile Properties Window   Layer Properties Window

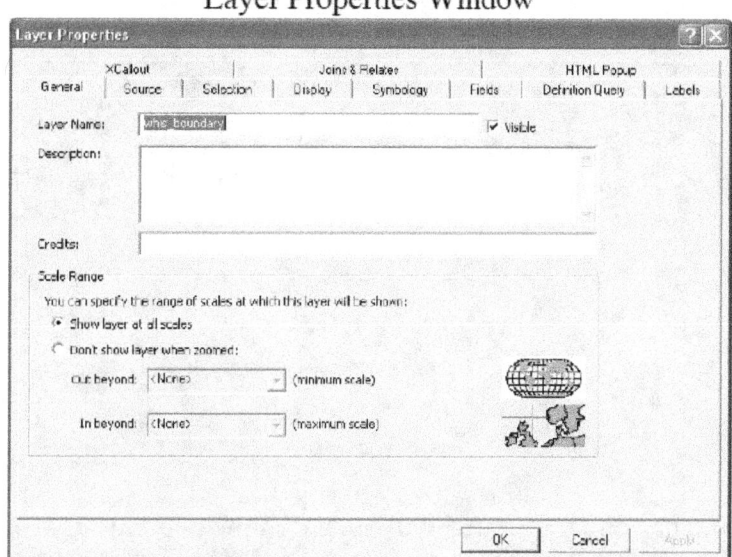

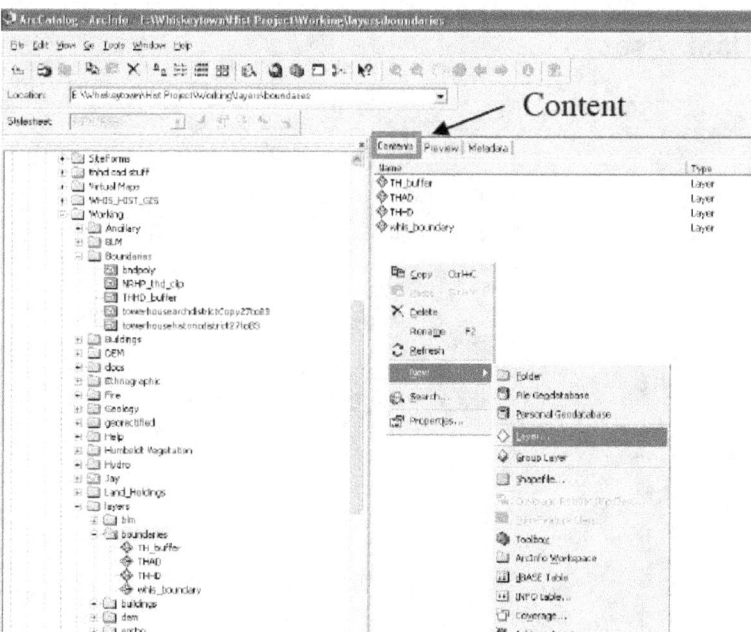

To open the Shapefile or Layer Properties Window, right click on the shapefile or layer file and select Properties.

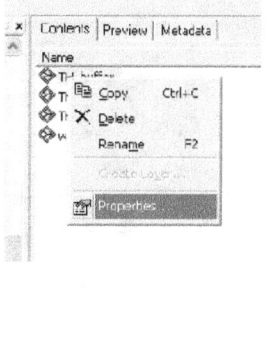

47

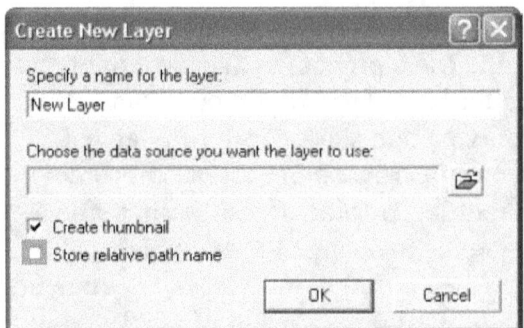

Selecting "Layer" opens the Create New Layer Window. Enter the name you wish to give the layer in the top box. Click the Browse button to open the Browse For Data window. Navigate to the location of the shapefile you are creating a layer for, select the shapefile and click Add. The Browse For Data window will close. Check the box next to **Store relative path name** and click OK.

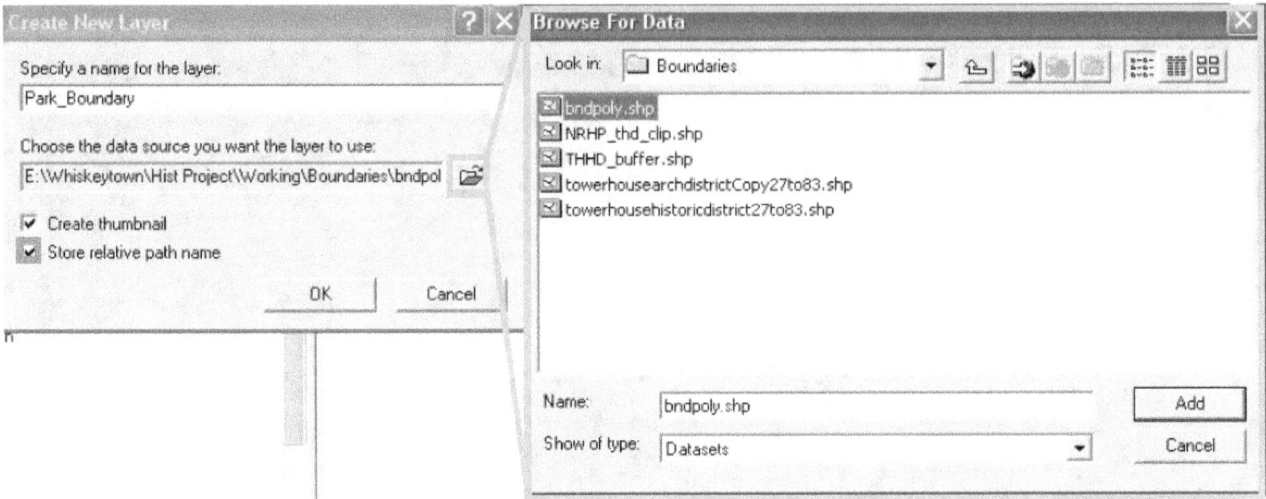

The layer you just created will appear in the content view of ArcCatalog and can be updated as you see fit.

Creating and Adding Data to Geodatabases

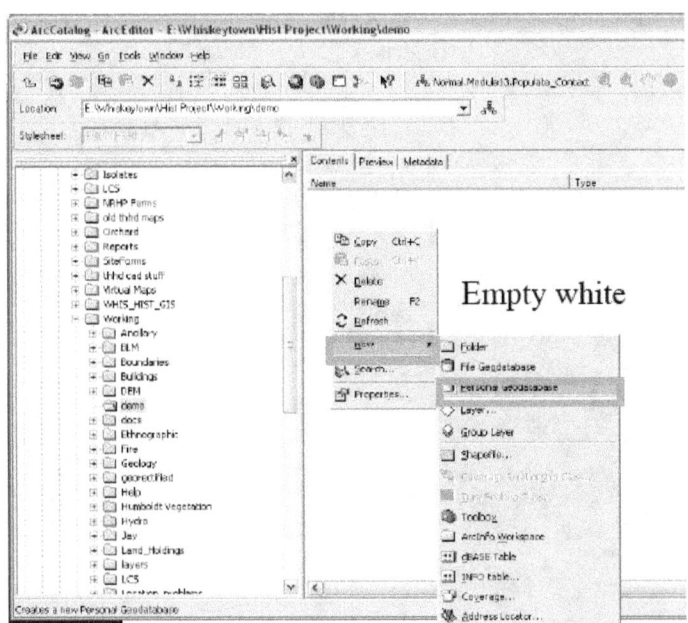

To create and add data to a geodatabase, right click in the empty white space of the folder where the geodatabase will be located. Select "New" and then select "Personal Geodatabase".

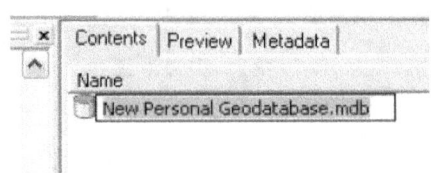

The geodatabase will appear in the folder with a default name. You are able to rename the file just as you would rename any other type of folder.

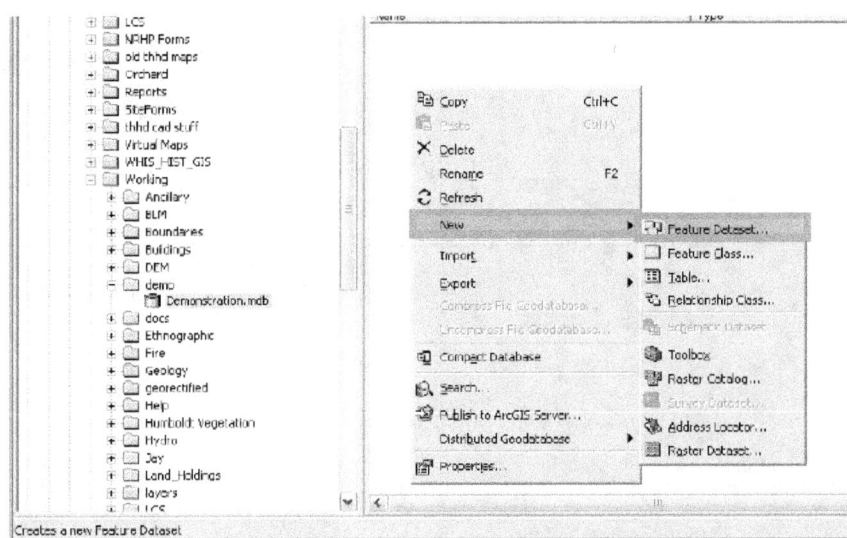

Click on the geodatabase in the folder tree. The contents of the geodatabase are displayed on the right. To add a dataset, right click in the empty white space, select "New", and select "Feature (Dataset)".

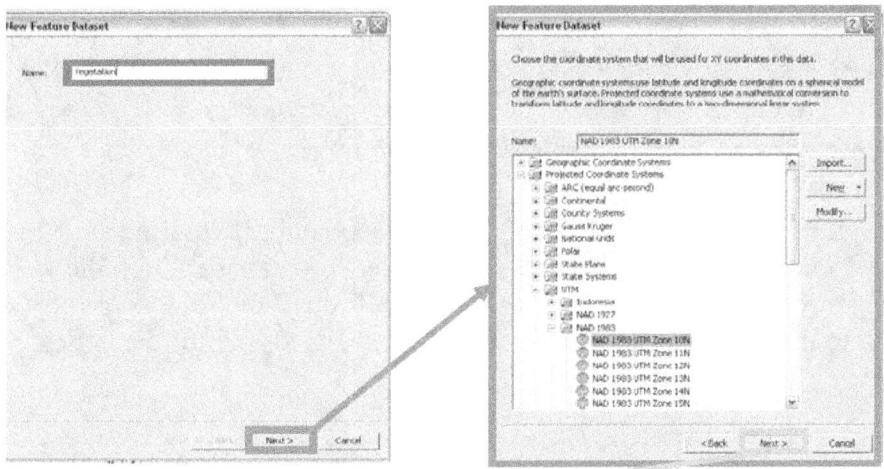

Selecting "Feature (Dataset)" opens the New Feature Dataset window series. Follow the steps to set up the feature dataset in the geodatabase. First enter a name for the dataset, click Next. Then second window requires you to choose an XY coordinate system for the dataset. Select the proper coordinate system to match the coordinate system of the data you will be importing. Click

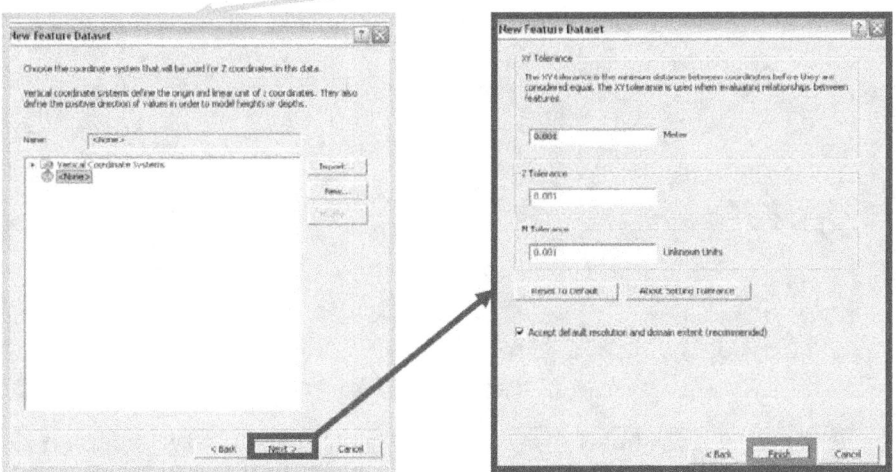

The third window asks for a Z coordinate system for the dataset. The dataset does not need Z coordinates. Select None and click Next. The fourth and final window asks for you to specify the XY tolerance of the coordinate system. This is also OK as is. Click Finish to complete the feature

The next step for adding data to a geodatabase is to import individual features to the newly created feature dataset.

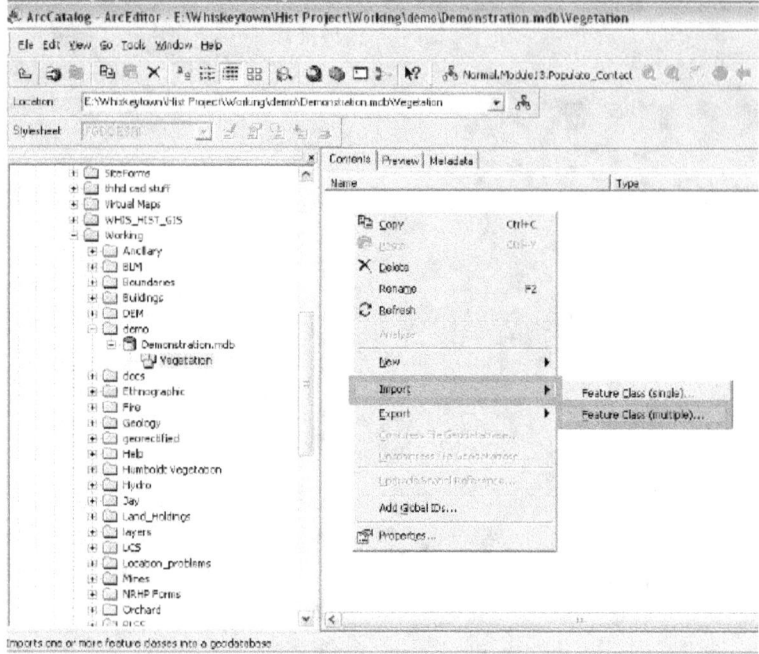

In the folder tree, select the feature dataset. In the content view, right click in the empty white space, select Import and then select "Feature Class (multiple)".

Selecting "Feature Class (multiple)" will open the Feature Class to Geodatabase (multiple) window. This window allows you to import multiple shapefiles to the geodatabase. Click the Browse button and the Input Features window will appear. Navigate through the folders to the location(s) of the data you wish to import. You select one or multiple files to import, then click Add.

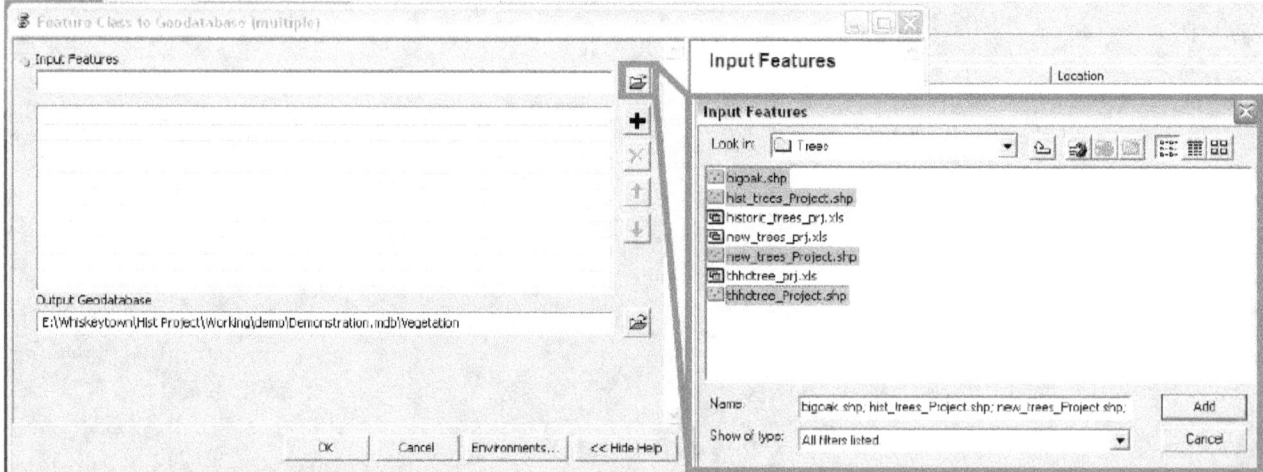

When you click Add, the Input Features window will disappear and the data you have selected will display listed in the Feature Class to Geodatabase window. Here you are able to rearrange the order of how the data will be displayed in the geodatabase by clicking on a file(s) listed and then clicking either the up arrow or down arrow buttons. You are also able to remove any unwanted files by clicking on the file and then clicking the X button. When you are satisfied with the order, click OK. Data can be added to the geodatabase at any time. If you forgot to add a file, you can always go back and add it without any trouble.

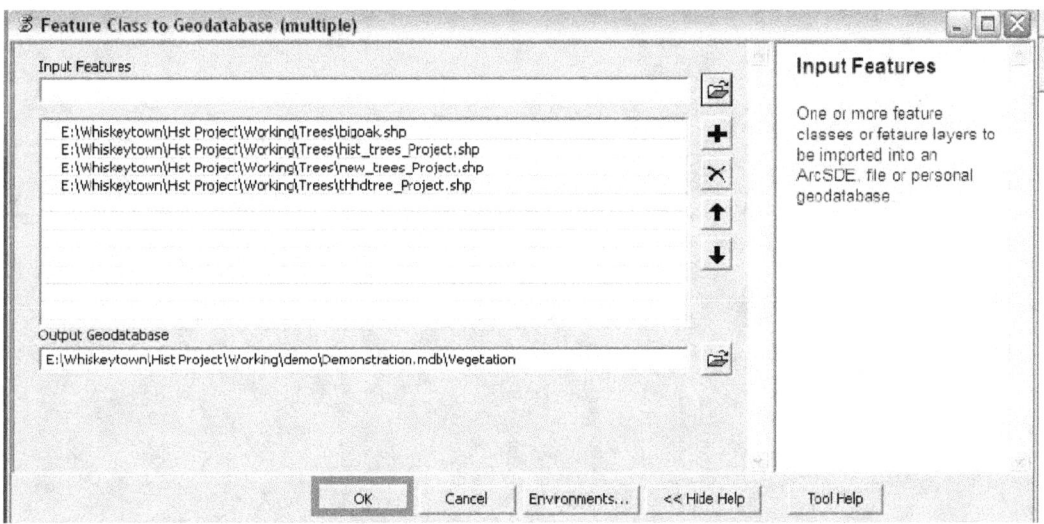

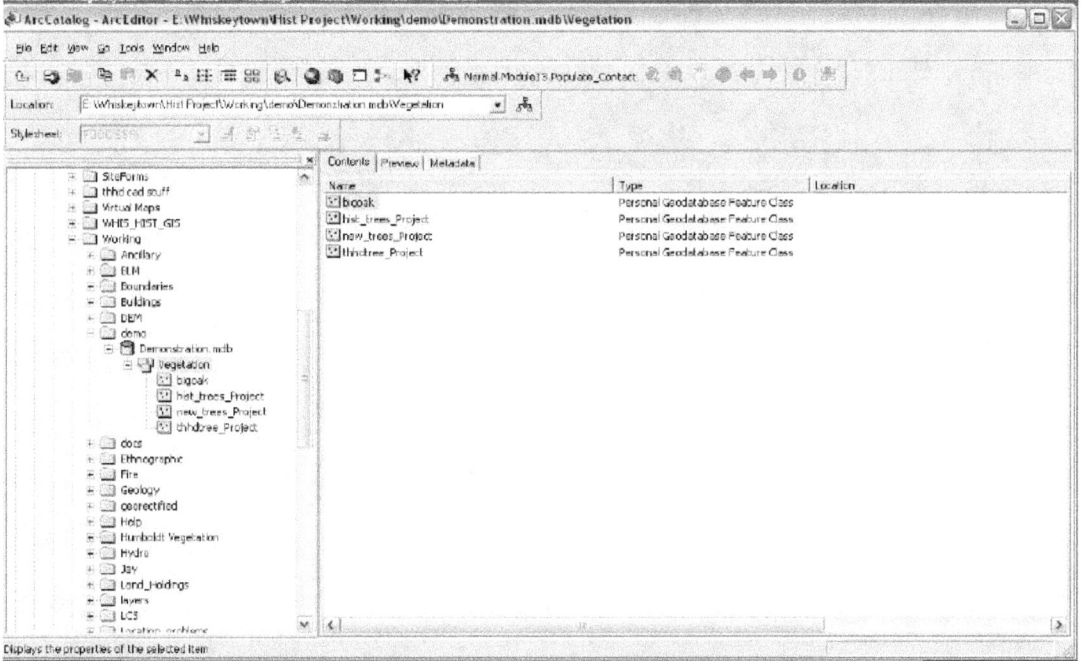

Now you have successfully created a geodatabase and added data to it. You can now add multiple datasets to your geodatabase and or create multiple geodatabases to meet all your data organization needs.

NPS 611/104871, July 2010